The GREATEST
in the WORLD

illustrated by
**Graham Kennedy**

Tony Rossiter

## The Greatest

# Retirement

## Tips in the World

A 'The Greatest in the World' book

www.thegreatestintheworld.com

Illustrations:
Graham Kennedy
gkillus@aol.com

Cover & layout design:
the designcouch
www.designcouch.co.uk

Cover images:
© Kevin Britland; © A C; © Vitalii Gubin;
© Fabienne Lerault; © Regien Paassen; © Lisa F Young
all courtesy of www.fotolia.com

Copy editor:
Bronwyn Robertson
www.theartsva.com

Series creator/editor:
Steve Brookes

Published in 2007 by
The Greatest in the World Ltd., PO Box 3182
Stratford-upon-Avon, Warwickshire CV37 7XW

Text and illustrations copyright © 2007 – The Greatest in the World Ltd.

A CIP catalogue record for this book is available from the British Library
ISBN 978-1-905151-28-8

Printed and bound in China by 1010 Printing International Ltd.

# RETIREMENT:
a time to do what you want to do, when you want to do it, where you want to do it, and how you want to do it.

*Catherine Pulsifier*

# Contents

# Introduction

I have really enjoyed writing this book. I hope you will enjoy reading it. It's not the kind of book you have to read from cover to cover. You can dip in and out – or just look at the chapters that interest you.

Retirement is one of life's great sea changes – like leaving home for the first time, or starting work, or getting married. Perhaps things will be different in the future. With more flexibility about the age of retirement, and the outlawing of age discrimination, it might become easier and more usual to retire earlier or later than the traditional 60 or 65 (by 2010 the state pension age for both men and women will be 65 – to be increased to 68 by 2044). And it might become much more common to combine retirement with part-time work. That's what I have been able to do, and I'm very lucky.

Many people look forward to retirement, but it does not always live up to their expectations. In fact, if you're not prepared for it, the reality can come as a shock. This book is intended to help you prepare for retirement; and, once you're retired, give you some information and suggestions that I hope you will find helpful. I can't guarantee that every single tip will work for you. All I can say is that I believe in them.

In an increasingly complex world, with so many baffling new developments, there is a lot to be said for keeping things simple. KISS – Keep It Short and Simple – is a good rule for many activities and areas of life. That's one reason I like the bite-sized format of The Greatest Tips in the World series. The other reason is the light, humorous writing style. If you're a very serious person, and you like to have masses of information and statistics and lots of complex arguments, there are plenty of long, serious books you can read. But if, like most of us, you prefer a light touch, simplicity and a little humour, this book is for you.

*Tony Rossiter*

"The stereotype of retirement as a time for pipe and slippers is outmoded. It's now a time for trying new things and having a new lease of life.

*Gordon Lishman*
Director General, Age Concern

# A new life

# chapter 1
# A new life

The days when retirement was seen as the fag-end of life are well and truly over. Nowadays retirement commonly lasts for 20 years or more – around half the amount of time most people spend in full-time work. And the concept of retirement itself is changing and becoming more flexible, with more people stopping work earlier or later than the traditional 60-65, and often combining retirement with part-time work.

Today, instead of seeing retirement as a time to wind down and stop doing things, more and more people see it as an opportunity to change gear and move on. It should be the beginning of an exciting new chapter of your life – a time to do all the things you have always wanted to do, but have never got around to.

Perhaps, above all, it is an opportunity to take stock of your life and to decide what you want to do with the time you have left. You'll want to make the most of it. To do that, you need to take a hard look at yourself; to decide what's important to you and what isn't; and to make sure you spend most of your time doing what you enjoy. Life, after all, is for living – especially when you're retired.

# "Retirement is wonderful. It's doing nothing without worrying about getting caught at it.

*Gene Perret*

## It's a new beginning

Think of retirement not as the tail-end of life, but as a new beginning. Look forward, not back. It's an opportunity to do all those things you always wanted to do but never quite got around to. As George Eliot put it "It is never too late to be what you might have been."

### Quick tip

**BEING YOU**

The chances are you've spent a lot of your life pleasing other people – especially those you worked for. Now you can show your true colours! Don't be bossed about. Take control of your life and spend your time doing things you want to do. It's a great opportunity. Don't waste it. Don't worry too much about what others think or what others expect of you. Be true to yourself.

## Sort out your priorities

Politics is all about priorities, so they say. Well, in my view, retirement is all about priorities. You need to decide what's important to you, and what isn't. We all have just a limited amount of time left. You'll want to make the most of it. So clear your mind, decide what your real interests and objectives are, and prioritise them. Then you can devote the majority of your time to the things that are most important to you.

## Stand still and take stock

Life expectancy rose dramatically in the 20th century – in the developed world, from 49 in 1900 to 75 in 2000. In 1950 the average life expectancy in the UK for a male aged 65 was 77 years. This has now increased to 84 years. Average life expectancy is now increasing by three months every year. If you retire at 60-65, the chances are that you've got another 20 years or so left. Of course you might live much longer than that; these days lots of people live into their nineties. In 30 years' time one in three 60-year olds will make it to 100! But it's the quality, not the length, of life that really matters. Retirement is a good time to take stock; it makes sense to review your health, your finances, how you spend your time, where you live – and how you're going to get the most out of the time you've got left.

## Rpm

No, not revs per minute – Routine, People, Meaning! Work has almost certainly given you three things that most of us need – apart from the money, which also comes in quite handy! These are: a daily routine, contact with people, and meaning to your life. Take these away, and you're left with three gaping holes. It's vital to find ways of filling these gaps. In retirement you'll need to establish a new daily routine and to find new ways of meeting people, and your life will need to have some kind of meaning; what that is will depend on you. You'll have to work it out for yourself. But it's important to have something to aim at in life – whether it's writing that best-selling novel, winning first prize in the local flower show, or being the best grandparent in the world.

# A new life
## Chapter summary

- Think of retirement as a new beginning.
- Take control of your life – be you!
- Sort out your priorities.
- Take stock of your life.
- Check your health.
- Review your finances.
- Reschedule how you spend your time.
- Maybe reconsider your living arrangements.
- Establish a new routine.

"There must be quite
a few things that
a hot bath won't cure,
but I don't know
many of them."

*Sylvia Plath, 1932–1963*

# Health

# chapter 2
# **Health**

As we get older, the process of ageing changes our bodies. There is nothing we can do about that. But there is a lot we can do to help us stay as healthy as we can for as long as we can. Whether or not we smoke, what (and how much) we eat and drink, and how much exercise we get – these can all make a huge difference.

The good news is that it is never too late. However clapped out your body might be, the chances are that it is not beyond repair! If you're really determined to change habits that are damaging to your health, you can reap the rewards within a relatively short time-scale - if you have the willpower to persevere.

Of course, a healthy lifestyle does not guarantee freedom from illness. If you do develop serious health problems, it's not sensible to ignore them. Ill health is bound to affect your ability to enjoy life. But it's not a good idea to develop an all-consuming preoccupation with your own health. Your family and your friends will probably find that very boring! It's much better to think and act positively, and to concentrate on getting as much enjoyment as you can out of life, whatever condition your body is in.

## Four things you can do to stay healthy

You'll have a better chance of staying healthy if you take action in four key areas. Here they are in order of importance. First, if you're a smoker, giving up the weed will do more than any other single thing to improve your health. Second, keep your consumption of alcohol moderate. Third, take regular exercise. Finally, watch your weight. Even if (perish the thought!) you've led a dissolute life, action in these four areas can work wonders on the most clapped-out body. You'll have a better chance of living long enough to enjoy your retirement.

## Stop smoking

There's no doubt about it. Smoking damages your health. It can cause or exacerbate all kinds of illnesses and diseases, from throat or lung cancer to breathing difficulties, bronchitis, and heart disease. Over 100,000 people in the UK are killed by smoking every year. It's also very expensive. So if you can bring yourself to give it up, you'll be doing yourself – and those who care about you – a big favour. You'll be healthier and you'll be better off financially. Remember that smoking in pubs, restaurants and other public buildings is now against the law. With no smoking increasingly the norm in public places, you will be better able to enjoy social activities such as the cinema, theatre, music, the arts, and eating out.

## Don't overdo the booze

Around 22,000 people are estimated to die in the UK every year as a result of drinking too much alcohol. If you habitually drink the equivalent of two pints of beer a day or more, watch it! You're not an alcoholic, of course, but your body might just be getting used to it. On the other hand, a little of what you fancy does you good! One small glass of red wine a day is positively good for you.

## Get some exercise – but enjoy it!

When it comes to exercise, there are two things to remember. First, to be of real benefit it needs to be taken regularly. Second, you must enjoy it. If you don't, sooner or later you'll give it up. So if you hate jogging (and I do!) don't choose it as the way to keep fit. There are lots and lots of other activities that are just as good for you.

### Quick tip

**DON'T MAKE EXCUSES!**
The very best form of exercise is something you really enjoy and can fit into your daily routine. Find something that does not disrupt your lifestyle too much. That way, once you have taken the plunge and made a start, you won't be tempted to find excuses for not keeping it up.

## Build up the amount of exercise you do

If you're starting a new activity from scratch, it's important to begin slowly and gradually build up the amount of time you exercise. This way, your body won't have too much of a shock! A gradual build-up of physical activity will make it easier for your body to adapt. If you feel discomfort, don't push yourself. Stop for a while and have a short rest. After a few weeks you'll be surprised at how much you can do without needing to rest, and you might be astonished at how much fitter you feel.

## Look after your heart

Exercise is very good for your heart. It helps to keep it strong and healthy. The heart is the muscle that pumps blood around the body. The stronger it is, the more blood it can pump with each beat, so your heart does not have to work so hard to do its job. Exercise is an important way of protecting yourself against heart disease. It lowers your blood pressure and reduces the risk of having a heart attack or stroke – two of the commonest causes of death. Coronary heart disease accounts for about one in four of all deaths in the UK. If you've had a heart attack or heart surgery, exercise might help to prevent further damage and help you return to leading a full and active life. However, if you've been in poor health, exercise can sometimes be dangerous: always seek – and follow – your doctor's advice.

"Give me a young man in whom there is something of the old, and an old man in whom there is something of the young. Guided so, a man may grow old in body but never in mind."

*Cicero, 106–43 B.C.*

## Exercise is good for your whole body

It's not only your heart that will benefit from exercise.
If you build up the amount of activity gradually, your body's suppleness, strength, and stamina will all improve.
Your muscles will become firmer and stronger and your lungs, as well as your heart, will function more efficiently.
Your liver and nervous system will benefit too.

### Quick tip

**EXERCISE IS WIN-WIN**

You simply can't lose. Exercise helps you to relax, to cope with stress and to sleep well at night. But, believe it or not, it also makes you feel good and gives you the energy to do other things. With regular exercise you can really enjoy life to the full. If that's not win-win, I don't know what is.

## Exercise isn't expensive

You don't need to join an expensive club, buy fashionable sportswear, go to costly keep-fit classes, buy an exercise machine, or turn your spare room into a miniature state-of-the-art gym. There are many activities that don't cost a penny. Three of the best things you can do to keep fit and healthy are three of the cheapest – walking, swimming, and cycling.

## Dress comfortably

Comfort is more important than fashion! If you're out in the rain, a waterproof hat comes in handy – or you might prefer an old-fashioned flat cap (as I do). Whatever the weather, it's a good idea to wear loose, comfortable clothes when you're exercising – and good quality training or walking shoes which give plenty of support to your heels and arches and have built-in shock absorption to protect your joints.

## Take stock of how much exercise you get

How much exercise do you get now? Think about how much physical activity you've had over the past week. How often have you done something for about half an hour that has made you slightly out of breath? That's the kind of activity you need in order to benefit from it. The chances are you are not doing enough. Try to think of exercise as something that's as natural as sleeping or eating and drinking.

## If you're in doubt about taking exercise, see your doctor

For most people, exercise is a good thing: full stop. But if you are very unfit or overweight, or you're recovering from an illness, including flu and chest infection, consult your doctor about what form of exercise is best for you. The same applies if you have heart disease, high blood pressure, arthritis or joint pain, back problems, or diabetes.

# How to build up your walking speed

If you're starting from scratch, here's a day-by-day plan to help you increase your pace gradually over a period of 8 weeks:

- First fortnight:
  leave home and walk at your normal pace for 5 minutes, timing yourself carefully. After 5 minutes, make the return journey, increasing your pace slightly. By the end of the fortnight aim to do the return journey in 4 minutes.

- Second fortnight:
  walk at your normal pace for 10 minutes. Increase your pace slightly on the homeward journey, aiming to do it in 9 minutes by the end of the fortnight.

- Third fortnight:
  walk at a brisk pace for 12 minutes. Increase the pace slightly on the return leg, aiming to do it in 11 minutes by the end of the fortnight.

- Fourth fortnight:
  walk for 12 minutes, alternating a brisk walk with your normal pace. On each homeward journey, increase the pace slightly.

# How to build up your swimming speed

Perhaps you prefer swimming to walking? You can still build up your stamina gradually. Here is an 8-week plan:

- First fortnight:
  swim across the width of the pool continuously for 5 minutes. Have a short breather and then try to do it again.

- Second fortnight:
  gradually increase the time to 10 minutes' continuous swimming.

- Third fortnight:
  increase this to 12 minutes' continuous swimming, working as hard as you can on the way out and more gently on the way back – i.e. one width fast, followed by one width slow, and so on for 12 minutes.

- Fourth fortnight:
  gradually increase the number of consecutive widths of fast swimming, and follow these with the same number of widths at a slower pace. For example, begin with 2 widths fast followed by two widths slow. After a while increase this to 3 fast followed by 3 slow, and so on.

## Take one unit of exercise three times a week

What is a unit of exercise? It's vigorous exercise that can take many forms: 20 minutes' jogging; walking between 3 and 3.5 miles in no more than an hour; swimming 6 lengths of a standard pool; an hour of energetic gardening, such as digging; or climbing 450 stairs! Do any of these things three times a week and you'll have a much better chance of avoiding a heart attack.

## Choose something that suits you – and get started!

Decide when and where you're going to do it. You might want to ask a friend to join you so that exercise becomes part of your social life. Set yourself realistic targets. Don't lose heart and give up if you don't succeed at first. If you find it difficult to set aside time for regular exercise, begin by fitting a little extra walking into your normal routine, for example, when you go to the shops. And when you're out why not make a point of using the stairs instead of a lift or escalator?

### Quick tip

**DON'T OVERDO IT**

Exercise does not have to mean strenuous sports or hyperactive, gut-wrenching workouts. Half an hour's moderate exercise a day can make all the difference. The vital thing is to keep it up on a regular basis. Little and often is a very good rule.

**TAKE A WALK IN THE COUNTRY**

Country walking is a wonderful way to keep fit. It's the ideal way to explore the countryside. You can do it at any time of the year. You can do it either on your own or with others. And you can easily combine it with other interests, such as botany, bird-watching, or local history. Why not plan a longish walk every weekend – and go somewhere different each time?

## Try a canal path

If your body can't cope with the ups and downs of the English countryside, there is an easy solution at hand. Make for your nearest canal. Wherever you live, the chances are that there is a canal within striking distance. Before they were supplanted by the railways, canals were the main means of transporting goods, but if you travel by road, they are often hidden from view – behind hedges, houses, factories, or warehouses.

The great thing about canals is that they don't do steep hills. If a towpath goes up or down, the slope is usually very gentle and manageable, and the surface is often firm and good for walking. So if you can't cope with hills – if your feet or your knees or your hips or your back have a decided preference for the horizontal – a canal path is the perfect place for a walk. If you are lucky you'll see plenty of wildlife. But the best thing of all about a canal path – any canal path – is that it's mainly flat.

## Take a ramble

Do you enjoy "walking for pleasure, either with or without a definite route"? If you do, you're a rambler, because that's the dictionary definition. It's a nice word, rambler. If you're new to rambling, The Ramblers' Association can help you to get started. It can provide information and advice and put you in touch with your local group. See the website: **www.ramblers.org.uk.**

## You can walk in town too

With traffic congestion getting worse and worse, it is often much easier to explore towns and cities on foot. You can avoid being stuck in traffic jams, you can save money on petrol and bus fares, and by exploring a town on foot, you can really get to know it. Not just the centre and the tourist attractions, but the whole town – from top to bottom, inside out.

## Don't dawdle too much

Of course, it all depends why you're out walking. You might want to take a gentle stroll just for the sheer pleasure of being out of doors and looking at beautiful countryside or interesting buildings. But if you're walking in order to keep fit, you really need to keep up a brisk pace. Aim to do a mile in about 15 minutes. If you can't manage that immediately, build up to it gradually.

# Do you like sport?

No, I don't mean fishing or playing snooker or watching football! I'm talking about the kind of sport that involves some physical exercise – games like tennis, squash, golf, table tennis, and cricket (though the way I play cricket these days does not involve too much exertion!). All these sports can be played by those who are not in the first flush of youth. Of course, you'll have to come to terms with the fact that you'll never make it at Wimbledon or Lord's!

## Quick tip

### KEEP YOUR BRAIN TICKING OVER

Mental health is at least as important as physical health. Your brain needs exercise just as much as your body. One way to get your mental faculties working in the morning is to begin the day with a puzzle. All the newspapers carry them these days, and they come in many different forms – for example, crosswords, sudoku, and those puzzles where you are given letters from which you have to form as many different words as you can. You should be able to find one that you enjoy. Don't choose a puzzle that you can do without thinking about it! You need something that compels you to get your brain working – but is not so difficult that you give up on it almost before you've begun. Puzzles can become addictive – but there are worse forms of addiction.

## Be a competitor

Entering competitions is another way to keep the brain in good order. There are many different kinds, run by many different organisations – from daily newspapers to radio and television shows, to companies selling everything from holidays to baking powder. And, just like puzzles, some are easier than others. They might test your general knowledge or your ability to compose a simple advertising slogan. Whatever it is you are asked to do, it will help to keep your brain in working order. And, you never know, you might even win a prize!

## Have your body MOT'd

Get your blood pressure and urine tested every three years. High blood pressure increases the risk of strokes. Have your eyes tested regularly too – every two years is good. If you're over 60, the test is free. And watch your cholesterol level; 5.5 is OK – anything over 7 needs dealing with, usually by taking more exercise or improving your diet.

## Watch your weight

If you're seriously overweight, it can lead to all kinds of health problems, including heart disease and high blood pressure. If you think you need to lose weight, ask your doctor to suggest an appropriate diet. There are a great many dietary regimes for losing weight, and they all have their advocates. Find one you can cope with that works for you. And stick with it.

## Get out the scales and the tape measure

Do you know what your body mass index (BMI) is? That's how doctors calculate whether or not you're overweight. It's not an entirely satisfactory measure, because it takes no account of the proportion of body fat to muscle, but it's a useful indicator. To calculate your BMI all you have to do is to divide your weight in kilograms by your height in metres squared. For example, if you weigh 50 kilograms and your height is 1.5 metres, you divide 50 by the square of 1.5 (i.e. 2.25) to arrive at your BMI – in this case, 22. A BMI count of 20 to 25 is considered normal, 25 to 29 is overweight, 30 to 39 is obese, and over 40 is severely or clinically obese.

## Eat less fat … and more fibre

Much of the food we love contains a lot of saturated fat. If you like sausages, meat pies or hamburgers, it's best not to overindulge. The same goes for any fried food, and for cakes, biscuits, and dairy products. They're all high in saturated fats, which increase the amount of cholesterol in the blood. So it's better to grill your food rather than fry it, use low-fat spreads, and choose vegetable cooking oils that are high in polyunsaturates. And eat less red meat and more chicken and fish. It's a good idea to fill up on food like pasta, potatoes, rice, and wholemeal bread. These are all rich in fibre. And you should eat at least five portions of fresh fruit or vegetables every day.

## Don't over-eat in the evening

If you want to avoid putting on weight, it's a good idea to have your main meal at lunchtime and just a light snack in the evening. Most of us are less active in the evening than during the rest of the day. If you're just sitting in an armchair or sleeping, what you've eaten will stay with you for longer and be more likely to increase your body weight. If you must have a heavy meal in the evening, remember the old proverb: "After dinner rest a while, after supper walk a mile."

## Don't forget Age Concern

Age Concern is a voluntary organisation that acts as an interest group, championing the welfare of older people and the promotion of local services. See the website: **www.ageconcern.org.uk.** It runs Heyday, a not-for-profit subscription organisation aimed at helping retired people to get the best out of life. See the website: **www.heyday.org.uk.**

## Quick tip

**WORK IS GOOD FOR YOU**

Statistics suggest that those who give up work completely are likely to die, on average, six years earlier than those who don't. Of course, once you're retired you'll want to spend time doing things you really enjoy. But if you want to live longer, it's not a bad idea to spend at least part of your time working.

# Get advice from Help the Aged

Help the Aged is a long-established voluntary organisation that provides help and support on health and other issues affecting older people. See the website: **www.helptheaged.org.uk.** It publishes the following free advice leaflets:

- Can You Claim It? (about claiming pension credit and other benefits)
- Check Your Tax
- Claiming Disability Benefits
- Questions on Pensions
- Thinking About Money
- Care Homes
- Fire
- Help in Your Home
- Housing Matters
- Keep Out the Cold
- Your Safety
- Your Security

- Bereavement
- Better Hearing
- Better Sight
- Bladder and Bowel Weakness
- Fight the Flu
- Fitter Feet
- Healthy Bones
- Healthy Eating
- Keeping Mobile
- Managing Your Medicines
- Shingles
- Staying Steady

# Health
## Chapter summary

- Stop smoking.
- Drink alcohol in moderation.
- Take regular exercise.
- Keep an eye on your weight.
- Eat sensibly – less fat and more fibre.
- Free advice leaflets are available from Help the Aged on many health issues including:

  *Better Hearing*

  *Better Sight*

  *Healthy Eating*

  *Keep Out the Cold*

  *Fight the Flu*

  *Bladder and Bowel Weakness*

> "The challenge of retirement is how to spend time without spending money."

*Anon*

# Money

# chapter 3
# **Money**

You'll enjoy your retirement more if you don't have to worry too much about money. The best advice is to plan ahead. Before you retire, take a good look at your financial resources; make an estimate of your post-retirement income and expenditure; and think about your future needs.

If things are going to be tight, consider ways of reducing your expenditure and increasing your income. Make sure you're getting a good return on any savings or investments. Look at ways of cutting down your regular outgoings. Consider looking for part-time work. Make sure you are getting your winter fuel payment and any other allowances to which you are entitled.

And remember that there are many good things in life that don't cost a penny!

## Retirement Wit

*Retirement: that's when you return from work one day and say, "Hi, Honey, I'm home – forever."*

## Remember that the best things in life are free

OK, most people need a decent basic standard of living: they need somewhere comfortable to live and enough food to eat. Beyond that, most people's happiness does not depend upon an ability to acquire more and more possessions. Look at the tabloids' stories of unhappy lottery winners, unable to handle their sudden wealth. Money does not make you happy. However, as my Aunt Una would say, if you've got some money, at least you can be miserable in comfort!

## Plan for retirement

Many companies run courses to prepare employees for retirement, and commercial one-day courses are also available. These often focus on financial planning for retirement. It's important to think ahead about what income and what outgoings you'll have after you've retired. A lot of information and advice is available covering such things as pensions, benefits, tax, and part-time work.

Visit the websites **www.direct.gov.uk/en/over50s** where there is a checklist of things you should do before you retire.

---

### Retirement Wit

*Middle age is that time when the broadness of the mind and the narrowness of the waist change places.*

---

# How to save both money and energy

You can save money and do something for the environment at the same time:

- 25cm (10″) of loft insulation can cut your heating costs by a third.

- Cavity wall insulation in the average house can reduce heating bills by £130–£160 a year.

- Energy-saving light bulbs can save £9 a year for each bulb.

- Replacing an old boiler could cut your heating costs by a third – and help to reduce $CO_2$ emissions.

- Using a cold wash cycle, at a temperature of 40°C rather than 60°C, means that you use a third less electricity. However, you should do at least one 60°C wash per week to reduce soap build up in the washing machine.

- Turning down the thermostat by 1°C (1.8°F) can reduce your bill by up to 10% per year.

- An energy-efficient fridge-freezer can save up to £45 a year.

- When you make a cup of tea, boil only the amount of water you need.

- Turn your television and computer off when they are not being used.

# If you haven't got it, don't spend it!

Charles Dickens' Mr Micawber got it right: "Annual income twenty pounds, annual expenditure nineteen pounds six, result happiness." Make sure your expenditure doesn't exceed your income. If you find you haven't enough money to live on, or to live as you want to live, there are just two solutions – unless you're lucky enough to win the lottery or you have a rich uncle who's very fond of you! You can reduce your expenditure. Or you can increase your income. It's as simple as that. The choice will depend on your circumstances – and your own character. Only you can decide. If you can manage to do both, so much the better.

## How to reduce your expenditure

Make a list of all your regular outgoings. Include utility bills, accommodation costs, food and drink, clothes, subscriptions, travel, entertainment, holidays, and anything else that involves regular expenditure. Now go through the list and identify something you can do without. If it's too painful to cut something out entirely, look for ways of reducing the frequency of your expenditure. Perhaps you can get by with a visit to the pub just six nights a week instead of seven!

---

## Retirement Wit

*Everyone has a photographic memory ... some just don't have film.*

---

## Keep an eye on your utility bills

It's worthwhile reviewing how much you pay for essential household services such as gas, electricity, and telephone. Since these services were privatised, suppliers have multiplied. Charges can vary significantly, depending on the supplier, your consumption, and the method of payment you choose. If the potential savings of switching from one supplier to another are negligible, you might decide that the inconvenience of changing is not worthwhile. But you should at least do the sums; you might be surprised at how much you can save.

## Get free banking and other financial services

Most banks operate free current accounts plus a range of free banking services including internet banking and direct debits. The majority of UK cash machines are also free to use. But others – often those found in service stations, pubs, and clubs – impose a surcharge, usually £1.50. Avoid these machines. If a machine is going to charge, you must be told; the Financial Services Authority can provide information and advice on financial topics including mortgages, pensions, credit cards, and insurance. For services such as free financial health checks, warnings about current scams, and to check that your financial adviser is officially recognised, visit the website: **www.moneymadeclear.fsa.gov.uk.**

> **Money is a blessing that is of no advantage to us except when we part with it.**

*Ambrose Bierce, 1842–1913*

## Quick access to your cash

If you're likely to need quick access to your money – perhaps to fund essential house repairs, or to bail out a son or daughter who needs financial help – the main options are banks and building societies. There is a bewildering range of savings accounts available, and financial institutions have a nasty habit of opening new accounts without advising their customers to transfer their savings out of an existing account which is paying less interest. So you need to be nimble on your feet. It pays to shop around, and to review your savings account(s) annually. Another option is premium savings bonds. They don't pay interest, but you could win one of the monthly £50 prizes. Obviously, the more bonds you have (the current maximum is £30,000), the greater your chances. And you might just win the million pound jackpot! Admittedly, the odds against this are huge – but not quite as huge as with the National Lottery!

## Invest wisely

In the (perhaps unlikely) event that you've got spare cash to invest, take expert advice. You need to decide whether you're looking for short-term gains or are prepared to invest for the longer term. In the latter case, you'll be advised to consider stocks and shares; property is another possibility. Some people invest in art or antiques, but these are usually only a good investment if you are buying the very best of its kind. You need to be knowledgeable about the market and to be really sure about what you are buying: fashions – and therefore market values – change, sometimes over a relatively short period of time.

## Don't buy what you don't really need or cannot afford

It's not always easy, in our consumer society, to resist temptation. It's easy to be seduced into buying something you can manage perfectly well without. All too often, we spend more than we really need to, or more than we can afford. Once you're retired, both your needs and your financial resources are likely to be different from when you were working. Don't overstretch yourself unnecessarily.

## Make use of your Council's free services

Council services vary across the country. In addition to collecting your rubbish, most provide a free pest control service (catching and disposing of rats, for example). Some also collect unwanted fridges and a limited number of bulky household items. Fire services will usually advise on safety awareness and smoke alarms, and test electric blankets (said to be responsible for 5,000 fires every year). Make full use of your Council's free services. After all, they're not really free! You've already paid for them through your Council Tax.

### Quick tip

**GET A SENIOR RAILCARD – AND A BUS PASS**
Once you reach 60, you're entitled to a senior railcard (the current cost is £20). For anyone who travels by rail, this is well worthwhile. As long as you avoid peak hours, you can get substantial reductions on the standard fare. Most counties also provide free bus passes to the over 60s.

## Try book swapping or book crossing

If you love reading but want to reduce the amount you spend on new books and recycle the books you've finished with, why not try book swapping? There is a free web-based book swapping service, **www.readitswapit.co.uk**, which provides thousands of books to choose from. Once registered, you can offer any books you've finished with as available to swap.
If you're a little more adventurous, and perhaps want to take a chance on discovering a hitherto unknown literary gem, you can try bookcrossing (a word that has entered the Oxford English Dictionary). Just leave your old book in a place where it's likely to be picked up by someone else. Coffee shops, trains, and park benches are favourite spots for this.
And be on the look-out for books which others have discarded. There's a website, **www.bookcrossing.com**, where you can track your book by writing an ID number in it enabling the person who finds it to log it back.

## Look out for cheap or free takeaways

You can stretch your budget by going along to the supermarket and buying food that is past, or very close to, its sell-by date – often sold off at a fraction of the original price. You need to be sensible about this: if what you buy makes you ill, it's not much of a bargain! Another well-known trick is to wait until the end of the day to go to the market so that you can pick up cheap fruit and veg the stallholder is keen to get rid of. It's also worth watching out for free tastings at supermarkets and posh department stores. Christmas is a particularly good time for this.

## Become a mystery shopper

If you're someone who enjoys shopping, why not become
a mystery shopper? You can get to try all kinds of goods
and services for free – and you can even keep some of them.
Sounds too good to be true? Well, there is a catch. You have
to provide feedback on the quality of service you receive.
And this is a serious business. You have to take notes and
carry out assignments to a high professional standard. Visit
the websites: **www.mystery-shoppers.co.uk** and
**www.retaileyes.co.uk** to find out more.

## Swap your skills

Whether it's repairing a leaking water pipe or dealing with a computer crash, getting the specific skills you need – and getting them quickly and at a reasonable cost – can be far from easy. Having the right personal contacts is often the key. It's not surprising that skill swapping is becoming increasingly popular. If you can provide something – anything, it doesn't matter what – that someone else needs, you can barter that for something you need. It's the way the world used to operate centuries ago. There are a number of skill-trading websites, including: **www.swapaskill.com**, **www.TeamUpHere.com** and **www.U-exchange.com** where you can post suggestions for a skill swap in your area. At another website, **www.timebanks.co.uk**, you can donate your time and skills and earn credits which can be exchanged for services from other individuals or community organisations.

## See how skills swaps work

Here are a few typical examples:

- Sewing curtains in return for childcare.
- Hedge trimming in return for help with computer problems.
- French lessons in return for house cleaning.
- Haircutting in return for car-washing.
- Yoga lessons in return for joinery.
- Cycle repair in return for car transport.
- Tree pruning in return for ironing shirts.
- Television installation/tuning in return for babysitting.
- Electrical work in return for website design.

# Recycle – and get stuff for free

If you want to get rid of things you can't use, help to reduce landfill, and have a chance of picking up something you need for free, there are plenty of networks that enable you to do just that. You can recycle unwanted items and request items you desire:

- Freecycle is a global network with 2.8 million users through which local recycling forums can be set up. You have to offer an item before you post a request. See the website: **www.freecycle.org**.

- Gumtree is a noticeboard site with bases in more than 30 cities in the UK and Ireland. See the website: **www.gumtree.com**.

- Free2Collect works on the principle that one person's rubbish is someone else's treasure. Unwanted items can be posted for others to claim – on condition that the claimant organises and pays for collection. See: **www.free2collect.co.uk**.

- Local Exchange Trading Systems (LETS) allows people to exchange both goods and services free of charge. Each service performed earns points that can be used to obtain goods or services from others. You must go along to an introductory meeting in order to join the scheme. See: **www.letslinkuk.org**.

## Waste not, want not

We live in a throwaway society. Many of the things we buy are disposable; if something breaks down, we tend to go out and buy a replacement. Repair is often uneconomic and we have got out of the habit of turning something old into something new. Fifty years ago 'make do and mend' was the norm: old sheets turned into new pillowcases; frayed shirt-collars replaced by cutting a piece from the tail of the shirt; string and brown paper meticulously preserved so that it could be used again; tins, boxes, cartons, and glass jars kept to use as containers; old underwear turned into dusters. When something no longer serves its original purpose, don't just throw it away. Think about using it for something else. You can save money – and maybe make a tiny contribution towards saving the planet.

## Reduce your shopping bill

Examine your shopping bill – food, household essentials, clothes, and so on. Value for money is the key. Compare prices, but make sure you're comparing like with like. Is the quality the same? Cheapest does not always mean best value. Watch out for special offers, such as 'buy one, get one free'. Buying in larger quantities can save you money, but not if having more of something only tempts you to use more than you otherwise would – or if you buy so much that it will still be there in the cupboard after you're dead and buried!

# Take a working holiday on a farm

If you fancy getting away from it all for a few weeks but you're hard up, you can enjoy some country air without paying a king's ransom. One smallholder in Scotland offers a week's free accommodation and food in return for "hard work with chickens, ducks, geese, plants, and a few sheep". Some small scale farms in the UK and abroad offer free board and lodging in return for manual labour. Keenness and the willingness to work hard are more important than experience. Many of these farms are linked together under the banner of World Wide Opportunities on Organic Farms (WWOOF).

See: www.wwoof.org.uk.

## Quick tip

**DON'T SPURN HOTEL FREEBIES**

For seasoned travellers and bored businessmen, scooping up the bars of soap, shampoo, bath foam, and so on from the en-suite bathroom into the toilet bag has long been a routine part of any trip. People who go away less frequently might have qualms about this. There is no need. You can take all the toiletries. You've already paid for them! The same goes for pens, notepads. and repair kits.

## Use charity shops

It's one of the most striking changes of the last 20 years: the proliferation of charity shops in our high streets. We should not be surprised. Where else can you do three worthwhile things at the same time? Save money. Help a good cause. And recycle stuff you no longer need. The range of organisations running charity shops is enormous, from local churches and hospices to national charities and international bodies like Oxfam. Whatever it is you need, a charity shop might have just the thing – at a fraction of the price you would pay for the same item if it were purchased new.

## Swap your rags

If what you're wearing has seen better days or you're just fed up with it, but you can't afford to buy new clothes, there's no need to despair. You can always rummage through one of the charity shops. Alternatively, you might want to try clothes swapping, which has recently become popular in the United States. Don't just dump your old clothes in the bin – in the UK a million tonnes of textiles go to landfill every year. Instead, recycle them – swap them. For details, check out these websites: **www.whatsmineisyours.com** and **www.swapstyle.com**.

Retirement Wit

*Seen it all, done it all. Can't remember most of it.*

## Save money when you go abroad

Most banks charge a fee for changing your money into foreign currency. They also charge a fee when you use your debit card abroad to purchase goods or to take cash out of an ATM. The one current exception is Nationwide's FlexAccount. The other way to avoid fees is to take local currency with you. There are a number of places which change currency without charging a fee. Currently these include: the Post Office, Lloyds TSB, Marks & Spencer, Barclays, Nationwide, Thomson, Thomas Cook and Travelex. But remember that exchange rates vary enormously; it's important to shop around.

### Quick tip

**GET FREE SOFTWARE FOR YOUR COMPUTER**

If you're into computers, it's worth looking at the free software programmes now available. These include operating systems, web browsers, email programmes, and much more. But you need to know what you're doing! If you're a novice when it comes to computers, you'll probably be better off sticking to commercial software, such as that developed by Microsoft.

# Forage for free food

When you're in the habit of a weekly trip to the supermarket, it's easy to forget how much free food there is just waiting to be garnered. If you know when and where to look, you can supplement your weekly shop with an astonishing variety of foods. You can search woods, hedgerows, roadsides, gardens, seaside, marshland, meadows, heathland, and even wasteground.

## Put your scrumping skills to good use

I'm not suggesting you break the law. But if you were the kind of kid who was not averse to the occasional foray into the neighbours' gardens, you can use the same skills to forage for blackberries, hazelnuts, and wilding apples. Towns are often as good as the countryside: the ground has not been smothered with chemicals. Canal towpaths and churchyards can be good places to look. Keep your eyes open for feral grapes, field mushrooms, and wild cherries.

## Start foraging in the spring

Spring is a good time to look for free food. Wild garlic can be found in woods and hedgerows. Nettles, growing on hedgebanks, wasteground or at the bottom of your garden, can be used to make nettle soup. The leaves of common sorrel, found in meadows, pastures, and grassy roadside verges, make a great lemony addition to salads or tangy soup. Sea lettuce, found on stones and rocks between the high- and low-tide marks on beaches, can be served raw, chopped up with soy sauce and rice vinegar.

## Summer is good too

Search in woods and hedgerows for raspberries, wild strawberries, and water mint. If you're at the seaside, look out for cranberries, sea kale and marsh samphire. Samphire makes a lovely snack just on its own (especially if you put vinegar on it!) or a tasty addition to a main course. Meadows and heathland are good for wild asparagus, coriander, bilberries, and wild thyme.

## Autumn is the season of mellow fruitfulness

Autumn is the time when foraging for fruit really comes into its own. Look in woods and hedgerows for sloes, wild plums, elderberries, wild cherries, rose-hips, and blackberries; also hazelnuts, sweet chestnuts, and many types of fungi. You can find walnuts in roadsides or gardens, fennel in marshland, and juniper berries, black mustard seeds and cloudberries in meadows and heathland.

## You can even forage in the depths of winter

Winter is not the best time for foraging, but it's not totally bereft of possibilities. Look out for watercress, goosegrass, oyster mushrooms, and dandelion.

### Retirement Wit

*The trouble with retirement is you never get a day off.*

## Watch out for opportunities for full or part-time work

Over 70% of respondents in a recent poll said that they were "actively seeking to recruit people between 55 and pension age" in order to fill their skills gaps. There is an increasing awareness that the experience and interpersonal skills of older workers can add real value to a company's operations, and can meet needs which might be beyond the capabilities of younger, less experienced employees. In seeking out opportunities for work, make the most of the skills and experience you have gained in previous employment (or in leisure activities).

### Quick tip

**GREEN FINGERS CAN BOOST YOUR INCOME**

Not everyone who has a garden has the time or the energy to keep it up to scratch. If you can mow a lawn, trim a hedge, or weed a flowerbed, there might be opportunities for you to earn some cash. Keep an eye on the postcard advertisements in newsagents' windows. If you're knowledgeable about plants and you really know what you're doing in the garden, you'll be in an even stronger position to obtain this kind of work.

## Remember that age discrimination against job applicants is now illegal

The Employment Equality (Age) Regulations, which came into force in the UK on 1 October 2006, prohibit job advertisements from stipulating or implying an ideal age of applicant unless there is an objective reason for this. But ageism won't disappear overnight. If you're looking for a job, it's a good idea to revamp your CV, removing any references which might 'date' you:

- don't include your date of birth.
- do include dates related to your work experience.
- don't put a date next to any academic qualifications.
- don't mention out-of-date qualifications such as O levels.
- don't mention obsolete IT systems.
- do put an email address on your CV.

## Some retailers like older workers

Since the mid-1990s a handful of enlightened customer-focused retailers in the UK, such as Asda and B&Q, have sought to recruit new staff from the over-fifties. The result has been an improvement in key performance areas such as staff turnover. The maturity and wisdom of people who have had some experience of life as well as of previous work can be of real benefit to both employers and customers.

"He neither drank, smoked nor rode a bicycle. He lived frugally, saved his money and died early, surrounded by greedy relatives. It was a great lesson to me."

*John Barrymore, 1882–1942*

## Work until you're 65 – if you want to

The new law sets the default retirement age at 65. Employers cannot ask their staff to retire before this age unless there are exceptional reasons for doing so. All employees must be informed at least six months before their retirement date. They have the right to request to work beyond this date, and if this request is refused a reason must be given. Anyone working beyond 65 retains full employment rights. Age discrimination is now illegal. Experts expect compensation claims based on age discrimination to amount to as much as all disability, sex, and race-discrimination claims combined!

### Quick tip

**GET HELP FINDING A JOB**

If you're over 50 and you're looking for a job (either full-time or part-time) help is available. New Deal 50 Plus is a government scheme providing people who are over 50 with support and advice on finding work. Consult your local Jobcentre.

## Start your own business

If you need both a source of regular income and something to keep you occupied in your retirement, why not consider starting your own business? If you work from home, your start-up expenditure might be minimal. A lot of help and advice – often including free training in key areas such as business planning, finance, market research and sales – is available from Business Link, local enterprise centres and Chambers of Commerce.

**Quick tip**

**DON'T FORGET TO CLAIM YOUR WINTER FUEL PAYMENT**
If you're over 60 you might be entitled to help with winter
fuel bills. The payment should be made automatically, but
if it has not been paid and you believe you are entitled to
it, check with the Department of Work and Pensions.

## The longer you can leave your money, the greater the return

If you can leave your money undisturbed for a minimum of five
or, better still, ten years, the range of investment opportunities
– and the potential returns – are much greater. It makes sense
to spread your investments, thus minimising the risks. If you
want near certainty – and, understandably, many people do
once they are retired – the returns will be less than if you are
prepared to countenance an element of risk. You'll need to
balance the potential rewards against the risks.

## Keep inheritance tax to a minimum

There is good news and there is bad news. The good news
is that you won't pay inheritance tax (you'll be dead).
The bad news is that your dependents will have to pick up
the tab. But there are perfectly legal ways of reducing liability
to inheritance tax. The most common is by setting up a Trust
into which the deceased's estate is paid. But the rules are
complex and it's important to get expert advice. Consult your
financial adviser and your solicitor.

## If you're good at DIY, don't keep it to yourself

Are you one of those people who enjoys decorating the house and is really good at DIY? If you are, you can use your skills to earn some cash. You can advertise by word of mouth, by putting a postcard in the window of your local newsagent, or by house-to-house distribution of a simple advertisement. Anyone who has a house knows just how much maintenance is involved – painting and decorating, routine repairs and renovations, carpentry, electrical and plumbing work. If you're a dab hand at any of these things, there are opportunities to turn your expertise into cash.

## Earn money by working part-time near where you live

A lot depends on what kind of work you're prepared to do – and how many hours you can work. But there are plenty of opportunities for part-time work and you might well be able to find something near where you live – especially if you are prepared to be flexible and to work at weekends or in the evening or early morning. Here are a few suggestions:

- Stacking shelves or working on the check-out desk in a supermarket.
- Driving a taxi or a delivery van.
- Behind the bar in your local pub.
- Serving in a local shop – look out especially for opportunities for shift work in shops with early or late opening, such as newsagents, cafés, off-licences, fish and chip shops, etc.
- Working in a petrol station.
- Delivering newspapers or advertising material.
- Working in your local Tourist Information Centre – or as a tourist guide, showing visitors around local places of historic interest.

## Retirement Wit

*Remember: Time flies like the wind but fruit flies like bananas.*

## Think of those you will leave behind

We don't like to think about death. But as the old proverb has it "nothing is certain but death and taxes". No-one is immortal. Just as you would plan for any major change (like getting married or moving house), it makes sense to plan for the time when you won't be around. Making things as easy as you can for those you will leave behind does not mean having an unhealthy preoccupation with your own death. It just means doing some simple things before you're on your deathbed. Make a Will. Put your financial affairs in order. Make a list of your bank and savings accounts, share holdings, insurance policies and so on, and deposit it with your solicitor. Make sure that other documents likely to be needed, such as your birth and marriage certificates, are in a safe place, and that someone knows where this is.

## Retirement Wit

*A woman walked up to a little old man sitting on a park bench, "I couldn't help noticing how happy you look," she said, "What's your secret for a long happy life?" "I smoke sixty cigarettes a day", he said, "I also drink seven bottles of whisky a week, eat fatty foods, and never exercise." "That's amazing", the woman said, "How old are you?"*

*"Twenty-six", he replied.*

# Money
## Chapter summary

- Plan for your financial needs in retirement.

- Make sure expenditure does not exceed income.

- Shop around for the best deal from a savings account.

- Consider ways of reducing regular outgoings.

- Don't buy what you don't need.

- Get a free bus pass and a senior railcard.

- Use charity shops.

- Swap your books, your unwanted items, and your skills on the internet.

- Forage for free food.

- Look for full- or part-time work.

- Consider starting your own business.

"Retirement is like a long vacation in Las Vegas. The goal is to enjoy it the fullest, but not so fully that you run out of money.

*Jonathan Clements*

# Friends & family

# chapter 4
# Friends & family

"There's nothing worth the wear of winning, but laughter and the love of friends" wrote Hilaire Belloc. Good friendships are one of life's greatest blessings.

Once you are retired, your friends are likely to be more important to you than ever. But, just like plants in the garden, friendships need to be tended and cared for if they are to survive and prosper. So take trouble over them, and don't take them for granted. Like many things in life, the more effort you put in, the more you are likely to get out.

Keep in regular touch with old friends, and go out of your way to make new ones – the more, the merrier: it's impossible to have too many friends. Of course, you'll be closer to some than to others.

Without work to worry about, you'll probably be able to devote more time to your family. Retirement is a good time to reassess their needs and expectations – and to think about your own.

## Retirement Wit

*If you can't be a good example, then … you'll just have to be a horrible warning.*

## Make sure your partner is prepared for your retirement!

If you have been used to being out of the house at work all week, and your spouse or partner has been used to being at home, (s)he might not find it easy having you around the house all day. The adjustment to the daily pattern of life might be just as difficult and problematic as it is for you. However well a couple get on, seeing one another only morning and evening and at the weekend is very different from being together all day, every day. For most people, it takes some getting used to. Try to plan ahead so that it does not come as too much of a shock! Communication is the key. Get him/her to think through in advance exactly what effect your retirement will have on him/her, and how (s)he will cope with this.

### Retirement Wit

*An elderly lady was driving around the M25 motorway when her hands-free mobile phone rang. Answering, she heard her husband's voice urgently warning her, "Margaret, I just heard on the news that there's a car going the wrong way on the M25. Please be careful!" "It's not just one car" she said, "It's hundreds of them!"*

## Speak to your partner about how you will spend your time

It's worthwhile thinking, before you retire, about how you intend to spend your days. If you've always had plenty of interests outside your work, you should not have any difficulty filling the time. If, on the other hand, you are one of those people whose life has revolved largely around their work, you might need to look at the Interests and Enthusiasms Chapter (page 80). Discuss your ideas and plans with your spouse or partner. Find out how (s)he feels about these and what effect they will have on him/her. Try to reach some kind of understanding, at least in very general terms, about how both of you will spend your time. Probably you'll want to spend some of your time together and some pursuing your separate interests.

## Quick tip

**KEEP IN TOUCH**

Once you stop working, it's easy to lose contact with the friends you made at work. Make a special effort to keep in touch. Arrange to meet up regularly. You can enjoy putting the world to rights, you can swap stories about former colleagues, and you can reminisce about your old boss and his non-existent leadership skills!

# Make an effort to make new friends

If you live on your own or if your life has revolved largely around your work, you might also want to make a special effort to make new friends. You'll have time to get to know the neighbours – if that's what you want to do! A good way to make new friends is to immerse yourself in some activity that you're really keen on, and to meet up, perhaps through a local club, with others who have the same interest.

# Don't be afraid of emails

Emails are a great way of keeping in touch with friends and relations. They're especially useful if your nearest and dearest are at the other end of the country – or on the other side of the world. Emails are cheap and they are easy to send and receive. If you have grandchildren, you'll be able to see digital photos of them as they grow up. But don't think of emails as a substitute for conversation. There are times when nothing but a one-to-one chat will do, either face to face or over the telephone.

# Nurture your friendships

For some, new friendships seem to materialise without effort, others might find it very difficult to get to know any new acquaintance. No doubt a psychologist could explain it all. Background and personality play a big part in how we react to others. Whether you find it easy or difficult to make new friends, it's worth putting some effort into it. You won't regret it. Like many other things in life, what you get out depends very much on what you put in. Put a lot of effort into making and keeping friends and you'll reap the benefits.

## You can mix and match your friends or keep them apart

It's good to have a wide range of friends with different backgrounds and interests. For example, you might have friends from school or university, from work, from a local sports club or other leisure activity, from a voluntary organisation you're involved with, and perhaps from your local pub or coffee-shop. Some people like to keep their friends in separate compartments. Perhaps you don't want people you're involved with through one activity to know too much about other aspects of your life. Or perhaps you feel, for one reason or another that friends from different circles would not get on well together. Fair enough. But sometimes people from very different backgrounds, with different interests and a different approach to life, can hit it off and get on amazingly well. So it could be fun to take a chance and get them together – and stand back and see what happens!

## Take time to think about your family

Families are strange things. Some are close-knit, and some are not. Some meet up regularly – perhaps to go on outings together or to celebrate birthdays or anniversaries. Others meet only for weddings and funerals and keep in touch only by exchanging an annual Christmas card. Most families probably have some people you get on with and see regularly, and others you don't see – and perhaps don't want to see – from one year to the next. In retirement you'll have the time and the opportunity to see more of your family and your distant relations – if that's what you want to do!

# "The only way to have a friend is to be one.

*R.W. Emerson, 1803–1882*

## Be a brilliant grandparent

It's not difficult to be a brilliant grandparent – all it needs is some of your time. Show an interest in whatever the sprogs are interested in – whether it's trains, or birds of prey, or some ghastly TV programme. Tell them stories about your own life (NOT too boring, please). Praise them. Love them. And, of course, give them the occasional – but not too occasional – treat.

## But don't undermine the parents

Being a grandparent is a lot easier than being a parent. You only see the kids for a limited amount of time. When things get difficult, you can hand the brats back! But it's important not to upset the way the parents are bringing them up. Don't let the children break their parents' rules or do things that you know the parents would not want them to do. Kids can be adept at playing grown-ups off against one another. Don't let them do it!

### Retirement Wit

*Give a man a fish and he will eat for a day. Teach a man to fish and he will sit in a boat all day drinking beer.*

# Friends & family
## Chapter summary

- Think about how your retirement will affect your partner.

- Agree a daily routine that suits both you and your partner.

- Keep in touch with friends from work.

- Make an effort to make new friends.

- Widen your circle of friends by joining local clubs that reflect your interests.

- Use emails to keep in touch.

- Enjoy your grandchildren.

"There are so many other interesting ways to spend your time. I feel like early retirement is a gift, but it's such an incredible gift. It's a gift I need to use."

*Martha Felt-Bardon*

# Interests & enthusiasms

chapter 5

# chapter 5
# Interests & enthusiasms

Retirement is the time to do all those things you love but were never able to do (or to spend enough time doing) while you were working. Be clear about your priorities – what are your real interests and enthusiasms? My idea of perfect bliss could be purgatory to you – and vice versa! Playing village cricket in the sun is pretty close to my idea of heaven. But my wife takes a very different view. The important thing is to have at least one consuming interest – something you're really passionate about.

You might want to spend more time on an activity you already enjoy. Or you might want to take up something completely new. It is never too late to learn a new skill or pursue a new interest. There have never been more adult learning opportunities – or more scope for doing voluntary work.

If you have a particular ambition – something you have always wanted to achieve – retirement could be the time to tackle it. You can get inspiration from the newspaper reports of people in their seventies who run their first marathon, or get their first novel published, or swim the Channel. Go for it!

## Anything will do

"I don't know how I ever found time to go to work" said a recently retired friend of mine. He had got stuck into his list of much delayed DIY and gardening jobs, and for the first time in his life he had been able to really go to town on his wide range of interests and enthusiasms. He's involved in all kinds of local activities. However, another friend who retired a couple of years ago has found himself at a loss, and has had great difficulty adapting. His life revolved around his work, and he never had much time or inclination for anything else. Without any consuming interests or enthusiasms, he has found it difficult to fill that gap. Boredom is the real enemy of retirement. When you retire, it's vital to have something to keep you going – something you're passionately interested in. As long as it's legal, it really does not matter what it is!

## Do it both together and separately!

Most people need companionship, but they also need their own space. If you're married or you have a partner, it's nice to have some interests of your own as well as some things you do together. I love cricket and writing. My wife volunteers for several organisations. We both enjoy bird-watching and country walking. You can get more out of life by spending time together when your interests coincide and doing your own thing when they differ.

**YOU'RE NEVER TOO OLD TO LEARN**

Retirement is a wonderful time to learn a new skill or take up a new hobby. The possibilities are limitless.

If you want to learn something new, you could begin by seeing what is available at your county's Adult Learning Centres (often located in schools or community centres): information should be available at your local library.

Fees vary, depending on the type and frequency of course, but they are generally modest. For example, if you live in Buckinghamshire and you're interested in digital photography, you could take a one-day course costing £25 or a 10-week course (one day a week) at a total cost of £72. And if you're on a low income you might be entitled to a reduced fee.

## Cast your net widely

Begin by thinking as broadly as possible about why you want to take a course. Do you want to learn specific skills that will help you to do a particular kind of work, either paid or voluntary? Are you interested in your own personal development – for example, your ability to handle stress or to speak in public? Do you want to learn a particular foreign language (perhaps because you're thinking of moving abroad or taking a holiday abroad)? Or do you simply want to take up a new interest?

# There are plenty of categories to choose from

My own county runs adult learning courses covering:

- English and maths.
- Foreign languages.
- Computing.
- Family learning and childcare.
- Skills for adults with learning difficulties.
- Personal development.
- General interest.
- Homes, gardens and interiors.
- Creative studies.
- Health, beauty and complementary therapies.
- Active lifestyles.

Here are some examples of the kind of courses available:

## English and maths

Courses at introductory through to advanced levels aiming to boost your confidence and, if you wish, to give you the opportunity to study for a nationally recognised qualification. There are also courses on Budgeting, Managing an Account and Taking Minutes for Business.

# English for speakers of other languages

Courses both for residents and for visitors to the UK. These provide the opportunity to practise speaking, listening, reading and writing in everyday situations. They help participants to develop the skills needed for work or at home with their families, for their own hobbies and interests, or on a visit to the UK.

# Foreign languages

Many different types of courses are available, at all levels from beginners through to advanced, in a wide range of languages: French, German, Spanish, Italian, Portuguese, Greek, Russian, Polish, Arabic, and Japanese. With modern teaching methods and technology, learning a language does not have to be a slog. You can learn in small, friendly groups with others whose knowledge is at a similar level to your own.

# Computing

If you're frightened of computers, or you find Information Technology a mystery, you can sign up for a Computers for the Terrified course. Lasting 8 weeks and costing just £20, it must be good value. A wide range of computer-related courses is available. Learn how to get to grips with email and the internet, how to create a weblog, or how to buy and sell goods on eBay. There are courses on word processing, spreadsheets, PowerPoint presentations, desktop publishing, and editing digital images.

## Family learning and childcare

If both you and your children or grandchildren want to learn a new skill, or take up a new hobby, together, there are family courses where you can do just that. There's plenty of choice: you can learn pottery, drawing and painting, badminton, squash, flower-arranging, yoga, jewellery-making, or line-dancing.

### Quick tip

**SKILLS FOR ADULTS WITH LEARNING DIFFICULTIES**
Plenty of choice here too, from literacy, numeracy, and citizenship through to cooking, art and craft, drama, dance, and gardening. There is even a one-day course on African drumming!

## Personal development

You're not the most confident or assertive person in the world? Don't worry: there are plenty of courses to help you become more self-confident and assertive. Your personal finances are in a muddle? Don't despair: sign on for the Sorting Out Your Finances course. You need to learn how to deal with difficult people? Don't give up: there's a course for that too. Whatever your particular need for personal development may be, the chances are that there is a course that will meet it.

# General interest

Genealogy, bridge, astronomy, psychology, archaeology, philosophy, creative writing – these are just a few examples of the many courses available. There are one-day courses to give you a taster and courses lasting 10 weeks or longer to give you a more substantial introduction to the subject.

# Homes, gardens and interiors

If you have to carry out essential repairs or home improvements, a DIY course might be just what you need. If you're planning more ambitious renovations, you can take a woodworking or even a bricklaying course. If your garden needs attention, you can learn garden planning and design or you can sign up for a practical gardening course. There are lots and lots of these, many of them leading to RHS qualifications and certificates. You can learn about interior design and soft furnishing. And if you need to brush up on your skills in the kitchen, there are cookery courses galore.

# Enjoy birdsong

It's one of the greatest musical performances of all time – and it's absolutely free. You can hear birdsong at most times of the year, but May is the best month of all. That's when the dawn chorus is at its peak. You'll need to get up very early to hear it in all its glory. Robins, blackbirds, and thrushes are usually the first to sing. With practice you can learn to identify these and other common garden birds, such as chaffinches, wrens and starlings, purely by their song.

"

None are
so old as those
who have outlived
enthusiasm.

*Henry David Thoreau, 1817–1862*

**CREATIVE STUDIES**

If your inclinations are artistic, you can take up life drawing, watercolour painting or textile art. Or you can take a 5-week art appreciation course. Alternatively, you might prefer woodcarving, pottery, working in stained glass, jewellery making, photography, embroidery, lace making, needlecraft, or patchwork and quilting. If music and dance is your thing, you can learn belly dancing, ballet, playing the guitar, singing in a choir, tap dancing or even salsa.

## Health, beauty and complementary therapies

If you want to keep your mind and body beautiful – or to help others do the same – you can learn hairdressing, massage, reflexology, aromatherapy, meditation, manicure, pedicure or Feng Shui. And if your house is in a mess, the Energy Clearing Your Home course might be just what you need.

## Active lifestyles

If sport and fitness is your scene, there are courses to help you get fit and courses to help you stay fit. There's a Gentle Exercise course and an Exercise and Dance course. There's a Ski Fit course and an Aerobic Workout course. You can learn badminton, tennis, yoga or Tai Chi.

## Consider other learning options

Adult education courses run by your County Council are not the only way to learn a new skill or study a new subject. Far from it. The range of options available is astounding. A lot depends on the subject you're interested in, the amount of time you can devote to it, and the level at which you want to study. You might want to see what the Open University has to offer; its teaching material is of a very high standard. Many other universities run part-time extramural courses, some of which lead to a degree. The WEA (Workers' Educational Association) runs a wide range of courses. My own local branch currently has courses on Byzantine art, Benjamin Britten, fossils, and modern China and Japan. These are held one day a week for between six and ten weeks, at a cost of £26–£40. A lot of help is also now available online: one good resource for learning in general, and language-learning in particular, is About (**www.about.com**), a website that covers hundreds of subjects. Its education section is especially good for French, Spanish, German, Italian, and Japanese. A lot of help is now available online. Try **www.about.com** and **www.language-learning-advisor.com.** The latter offers links for a huge number of languages.

---

Retirement Wit

*If you look like your passport picture, you probably need the holiday.*

---

# Visit a museum

Museums are no longer the dry, boring places they once were. Since entry charges to England's national museums and galleries were abolished, attendances have almost doubled. London's world-class museums (British Museum, V&A, Natural History Museum, Science Museum, National Gallery, Tate Britain and Tate Modern) are well known, but smaller provincial and specialist museums can provide surprising riches.

In Leicester's New Walk Museum and Art Gallery you come face to face with dinosaurs and creepy-crawlies, and children can explore the museum's interactive natural history section. The National Railway Museum in York is a treasure trove not only for trainspotters and railway buffs, but for anyone interested in the history of transport and the railways.

At St Fagans open-air Natural History Museum near Cardiff you can see a recreated model town of Welsh daily life throughout history. In Cambridge, Kettle's Yard, the former home of ex-Tate curator "Jim" Ede, is a special place with a unique art collection.

# Use the library

Don't overlook your local library. With only 9% of increased national funding for libraries being spent on new books, they may not be the force they once were, but even if you don't need to borrow a book, you can spend a peaceful hour or two thumbing through a newspaper or looking at a magazine. And the library is an excellent place for finding out what's going on locally – information about local groups, adult learning courses, music and drama, and other local activities.

## Find out what's going on locally – you might be surprised

My own local library currently has notices on display seeking new recruits for the following activities:

- bowls
- yoga
- horticulture
- line dancing
- beekeeping
- pottery
- Scottish country dancing
- hockey
- art
- choral singing
- cricket
- Irish country dancing

## Join a reading group

If you enjoy reading, you might want to join a local group where you can compare your impressions and opinions of a book you've read with those of others who have read the same book. Over the last few years reading groups have become increasingly popular. Many of them meet once a month. The usual practice is for members to take it in turn to choose a book which everyone undertakes to read before the group's next meeting. To locate your nearest group, see the website: **www.readinggroups.peoplesnetwork.gov.uk**.

# Or a writing group

If you've always felt that you have a book in you (and many people do), why not have a go at turning your dream into reality? Now that you're retired, you have a lifetime's experience to draw on – and the time to get it down on paper. You don't need to be brilliant at English. All you need is something to write about – and the perseverance to turn your raw material into a publishable book. That's not easy, but there's plenty of help available. Some people enjoy writing just for pleasure, perhaps wanting to leave some record of their life for their children or grandchildren. If you join a writing group, you'll be able to get feedback on what you've written, and you'll be able to benefit from the experience of other members. Most writing groups have a mixed membership, including both published and unpublished writers, and cover almost every conceivable type of writing. Whatever your interest is – non-fiction, poetry, crime, romance, fantasy, science fiction, biography, history, or anything else – joining a writing group could give you the kick-start you need.

## Retirement Wit

*My mother started walking five miles a day when she was 60. Now she's 97 years old and we don't know where the hell she is.*

## Don't be afraid of the internet – but be careful

The internet is like many other things in life, from television to alcohol. If you use it sensibly, it can add to your enjoyment. If you misuse it or you become addicted to it, it can make your life a misery. The amount of information available is truly astonishing. And that is one of the problems. Type any subject that interests you into a search engine, and you might well be shown over a million relevant websites. Too much information can be worse than too little: it makes it all the harder to find the specific thing you're looking for. Moreover, just because something appears on a website, it does not mean that it's true. If you're in any doubt, check your facts out with several different information sources. The internet is a tool: like any other tool, it needs to be used properly.

## It can be really useful

If you bear those two caveats in mind (the huge amount of information that's out there, and its potential unreliability), the internet can be extraordinarily useful. If you want to find something out, or you're undertaking any kind of research (from family history to the breeding habits of the wild Bactrian camel), it can save you an enormous amount of time and effort. And you can use it to book your holiday, make a theatre reservation, or do your shopping.

"Planning to retire?
Before you do find
your hidden passion,
do the thing that
you have always
wanted to do."

*Catherine Pulsifer*

# Go to an auction

Auctions can be great fun. If you visit a country auction in a market town you can, if you're lucky, pick up a genuine antique – or just a useful piece of second-hand furniture – for much less than you would have to pay in a shop. It's important to view beforehand. If an object is of interest, inspect it thoroughly (if necessary ask questions) and set yourself an upper limit before you bid. Items going under the hammer at posh London auction houses might be out of your reach, but works of art coming up for sale there – including some valued at millions of pounds – can be viewed for free if you go along to the viewings held at the London premises of Christie's and other well-known houses (smartly dressed, of course!). Once sold, some of these paintings might never go on free public view again.

## Quick tip

**VISIT AN ANCIENT SITE**

Britain has some amazing examples of ancient environmental sculpture that you can visit for free. There are Celtic crosses in the Welsh hills, chambered tombs in Anglesey, chalk figures in the South of England, and the long earthwork of Offa's Dyke. Look at the English Heritage and CADW websites:
**www.english-heritage.org.uk** and **www.cadw.wales.gov.uk**.

## Enjoy free art out of doors

Some of the best and most famous recent works of art are public monuments and can be seen in town squares and other public spaces. If you drive north towards Scotland on the A1 you can hardly fail to see the Angel of the North at Gateshead. Or you can enjoy Antony Gormley's Merseyside figures. One of the most striking pieces of modern art is often mistaken for rusting metal left by construction workers. It is Richard Serra's twisting tower of propped slabs of steel, on view outside Liverpool Street Station in London.

### Quick tip

**GO DANCING**

Ballroom dancing might be less popular than it was fifty years ago, but it seems to be undergoing something of a resurgence. Many clubs and other organisations put on regular sessions, and if you want to brush up your footwork, courses are often available.

## Play cards

Some people love playing cards, while others hate it. If you're in the former category, most towns and villages have clubs that cater for this interest with regular sessions of bridge or whist. Who knows, you might even find a poker club! If you've never had time for bridge in the past and want to learn from scratch, many adult learning centres run courses for beginners.

## Take part in a pub quiz

If you fancy the challenge of testing your general knowledge, and you enjoy a convivial drink, why not form a team to take part in your local pub's weekly quiz? The type of questions vary a good deal (though football and television programmes are probably among the most popular). The most successful teams have members with complementary knowledge. For example, one person might specialise in sport, another in music, another in television or cinema, and a fourth in history or politics.

## Get the board games out

When it's cold and dark outside and there's nothing worthwhile on television, why not settle down to a quiet game of dominoes or draughts? They are nice, easy-going games. If you like words, you can get out the scrabble board. And if you want to get your brain really working, reach for the chess set.

## Be in a studio audience

If you enjoy television or radio shows, you can apply for free tickets to BBC and other shows. Most are filmed in London, but some tickets are available for shows recorded in other areas such as Manchester or Birmingham. For details, visit the BBC, ITV or Channel 4 websites; **www.chortle.co.uk** is a website that lists free tickets currently available for comedy shows on both TV and radio and provides links.

# Don't be afraid to volunteer

There are more voluntary organisations in the UK than anywhere else in the world. You can use the experience and skills you've already got. Or you can branch out into something new – perhaps something for which you need to learn new skills. The choice is yours. Volunteers usually have their travel and other essential costs reimbursed; and if special skills are required free training might be provided.

## Volunteer for something you're passionate about

If you can volunteer for something you feel really passionate about, so much the better. The range of opportunities is astounding. Wherever you live, you should be able to find a volunteering activity nearby that matches your interests and abilities. Look at the information in your local library, call the National Centre for Volunteering (0845 305 6979) or go to the website **www.volunteering.org.uk**.

## Drive someone to the theatre and get in free

If you live in London and you enjoy seeing plays or going to the opera, you can volunteer to drive elderly or disabled people to West End theatre productions. In return, the Shape Ticket Scheme will give you a free ticket and reimburse your petrol costs. For details, see the website **www.shapearts.org.uk/shapetickets**.

# Research your family history

If you're curious to know where you came from, why not research your family history? It's a fascinating and increasingly popular hobby. There's plenty of help available to help get you started – magazines, books (such as *The Greatest Genealogy Tips in the World*) and websites. The General Register Office (part of the Office for National Statistics) can provide copies of certificates of birth, marriage and death. Parish church records and local newspapers are another great source of information. Who knows what you might discover if you look far enough back and you dig deep enough? Aristocratic blood? Someone whose name you remember from your school history books? Or a black sheep of the family who got involved in things no-one has ever wanted to talk about?

# Get interested in local history

If you'd rather not know who your ancestors were and what they got up to, how about researching the history of where you live? You could delve into the past of the town or village you live in, finding out how it began and how it grew to be the place it is today. Or you could look into the history of one aspect of local life that interests you, whether it's the cricket club, the WI, or the local pub. Or if you live in an old house you could investigate its past and the people who lived there before you. Who knows what you might discover!

# Get to know your own country

Retirement is a great opportunity to see parts of the country you've never visited – or parts you would like to get to know better. The climate might be unreliable, but from John O'Groats to Land's End, the range of scenery is astounding. Travel need not break the bank. Look out for special offers, out-of-season packages, and reduced rates for oldies.

# Get out into the countryside

The Countryside and Rights of Way Act 2000 gives you the right to walk and enjoy informal recreation on designated open access land. You're allowed to walk, sightsee, picnic, bird-watch and run. You can't camp, hang-glide, paraglide, light fires, or use a metal detector – nor can you cycle or horse-ride (except on bridleways and byways crossing access land). Walking on this land is different from walking on public rights of way. You don't have to stick to a defined line; you are free to explore whatever features interest you, and you can decide your own route.

## Quick tip

**IF YOU TAKE YOUR DOG, ACT RESPONSIBLY**
Rights on access land extend to walking with dogs. But between 1 March and 31 July – the breeding season for birds – you must keep your dog on a fixed lead of no more than 2 metres in length. The same restriction applies, throughout the year, whenever livestock are present.

"If you would be happy for a week take a wife; if you would be happy for a month kill a pig; but if you would be happy all your life plant a garden."

*Proverb, mid 17th century*

## Take a holiday – and try something new

If you fancy a holiday, these days you can be spoilt for choice. The range of possibilities is enormous. There is something for everyone – from the traditional seaside holiday to package tours to every destination under the sun. If you're an oldie and you like to spend your holiday with other oldies, you can do that. If you prefer to be with people who share a special interest of some kind – whether it's tasting wine or painting watercolours or even playing the bagpipes – the chances are that someone, somewhere, will be able to organise it.

## Get on your bike!

Cycling is good – for you, for the environment, and for your pocket. It helps you to keep fit. Using the bike instead of a car helps to reduce $CO_2$ emissions. And once you've got your bike, it costs next to nothing to maintain. If you need help, there's plenty available – and it's often free. Some councils offer free cycle safety checks – often during Bike Week (when some councils also host free cyclists' breakfasts to encourage people to ride to work). Some councils run free cycle maintenance courses, and if you live in London, Transport for London can provide a list of free maintenance workshops – great for getting old bikes back on the road. If you don't own a bike, you might be able to pay a deposit and borrow one for free, as you can with OYBike (**www.oybike.com**) in London.

# Try birdwatching – it's a brilliant hobby

The great thing about birdwatching is that you can do it almost anywhere and at any time of the year. You don't need to be an expert. All you need is your eyes – and, for those birds that don't oblige by coming near enough to be seen clearly with the naked eye, a pair of binoculars. You don't need to trek out into the countryside. Believe it or not, a small suburban garden is one of the very best places for birdwatching. You can put birdseed in a feeder to attract tits and goldfinches, and on the ground for blackbirds and dunnocks.

# Visit an RSPB reserve

The RSPB has nature reserves all over the country. You can get a good view of the birds and there is usually a reception area where you can find out about local species and recent sightings, buy books and leaflets, buy or hire binoculars, and get a cup of tea. There is a modest entrance fee, but entry is free to RSPB members. One of the most spectacular sites is Bempton Cliffs in Yorkshire, where in summer you can see breeding sea birds such as gannets, guillemots, razorbills, fulmars, and puffins. With over one million members, the RSPB is one of the largest voluntary organisations in the UK. For details of RSPB membership and RSPB nature reserves, see the website: **www.rspb.org.uk**.

## Four ways of saving money when you go on holiday

Believe it or not, a holiday need not cost you the earth. Here are four simple ways you can save money – without spending the night under canvas or in the grottiest of B&Bs:

- Watch out for special out-of-season holiday deals.

   Not so long ago my aunt and uncle used to spend a month of every winter on the Costa del Sol in Spain. With the saving on their winter heating bills, they maintained that it cost little more than spending the month at home in England.

- Swap your home

  Swap for a few weeks with someone who lives somewhere you've always wanted to visit! Yes, it is possible. It's an obvious way of keeping costs down. All you'll have to pay are your travel costs and normal living expenses. Of course, the quid pro quo is that you'll have to let someone else spend their holiday in your house. It's important to have a clear understanding of exactly what you'll be getting and what you'll be providing in terms of domestic and other facilities. Try these websites: **www.Geenee.com** (includes houses mainly in North America, the UK, France, and Australia); and **www.Homebase-hols.com.**

- Keep an eye on rates of exchange.

  At the time of writing, the pound is strong, the dollar is weak, and you can get plenty of dollars for your pounds. So the United States is a remarkably cheap holiday destination.

- Find out about the local cost of living.

  Exchange rates apart, the cost of living in many parts of the world is a lot cheaper than it is in the UK. If you go to the States, you can eat heartily without it costing you a fortune. In many parts of Central and Eastern Europe you can eat (and drink!) very well and very cheaply.

## See birds of prey from the motorway

It's not difficult to see kestrels, the commonest bird of prey in Britain. You can often spot them hovering above roadside verges, watching for a vole or a field mouse. Buzzards, too, can be seen fairly easily especially in western parts of Britain. I live in the Chilterns and the sight I like best is the result of one of the great conservation success stories of the last 20 years: the reintroduction into England of Red Kites. You can often see them from the M40 motorway where it crosses the Chiltern escarpment. They hang on the wind effortlessly, constantly twisting their distinctive, rusty-red forked tails: a magnificent spectacle.

## Visit a Wildlife Trust nature reserve

There are 47 regional Wildlife Trusts across the UK managing an amazing 2,500 nature reserves. The Trusts exist to create a better future for wildlife and are concerned with all aspects of nature conservation. Most of the Trusts' reserves are open to the public and provide excellent opportunities for watching wildlife. Activities include guided walks, illustrated talks, and other events to help people find out about wildlife and nature conservation. For more details visit the website: www.wildlifetrusts.org.

### Retirement Wit

*Light travels faster than sound. This is why some people appear bright until you hear them speak.*

## Take a wildlife walk

If you want to watch wildlife and get some exercise at the same time, take a walk in one of the Wildlife Trusts' nature reserves. Over 500 of these are described in the Trusts' publication *Wildlife Walks* (Think Publishing). This estimates the time needed for a full walk and also gives details of where to go and what to see if you can manage only a 30-minute visit.

## See rutting deer

One of nature's most memorable spectacles is the sight of rutting deer. It's not as difficult to witness as you might think. Head for Richmond Park, on the south-west edge of London, in early October, and get there at daybreak for the best displays. They are so used to people that it's possible to park your car and get quite close; but back off slowly (don't run) if a deer starts to stare you down! If you live miles away from London, the deer parks of some of our stately homes are another place where you might be able to see this spectacular sight.

## Take a literary walk

If you're interested in books and literature, why not follow the trail of your favourite writer? Go down to Dorset and follow in the footsteps of Thomas Hardy's tragic heroine, Tess. Go up to the Lake District, retrace the steps of that prodigious poet and fell-walker William Wordsworth, or explore Coniston Water, the setting for *Swallows and Amazons*. Or head for the coast of north Norfolk, where you can relive scenes from Jack Higgins' *The Eagle Has Landed*. The National Trust's publication *On the Writer's Trail* gives details of these and other literary walks.

## Visit a National Trust property

The National Trust owns hundreds of historic buildings, dating from the Middle Ages to modern times, throughout England, Wales and Northern Ireland (north of the border the National Trust for Scotland fulfils the same role). These range from grand estates, such as Waddesdon Manor in Buckinghamshire, to family houses, such as No 2, Willow Road, Hampstead, a 1930s Modernist house designed by Ernö Goldfinger. For details of National Trust properties, see the National Trust Handbook or visit the website: **www.nationaltrust.org.uk**.

## Explore National Trust land

The National Trust owns over 252,000 hectares (623,000 acres) of land of outstanding natural beauty and over 700 miles of coastline. There are magnificent walks, many with breathtaking views. Whether you want to ramble over hills, find an unspoilt beach, take a woodland walk, amble along a quiet riverbank or explore a coastal path, you're unlikely to be disappointed. The more popular beauty spots have car parks (sometimes with charges for non-members).

> ## Retirement Wit
> *The shinbone is a device for finding furniture.*

# Go to a music festival

Whatever kind of music you like – jazz, folk, classical, rhythm and blues, country and western or even pop – you're sure to be able to find a festival that caters for your taste. Some festivals are free and some are not, and many put on a mixture of free events and performances for which you have to pay. There are big national (and often expensive) festivals such as Glastonbury and small-scale local festivals, often centred on a church or community centre. Whatever kind of music festival you choose, the chances are that you'll find that special buzz you only get when people who share the same passion come together.

# Try a book festival

Nowadays – if you had the money, the time and the inclination – you could probably spend every weekend of the year attending a book festival somewhere in the UK. Places like Cheltenham, Hay-on-Wye, and Oxford put on annual sponsored events that attract large crowds and best-selling authors. And there are smaller festivals with lesser-known writers, sometimes focussing on a specific theme, subject or type of book. Most book festivals cover a range of genres and include talks by authors, with an opportunity for discussion.

# Or an arts festival

If your cultural tastes are eclectic, you might prefer an arts festival that covers the performing and visual arts, as well as literature. The Edinburgh Festival (and its famous Fringe) is the best-known, but also the most crowded. There are many others up and down the country.

## Visit a local garden

If you enjoy flowers and gardens, why not take advantage of the National Gardens Scheme? Every summer scores of people open their gardens to the public for one day (usually a Sunday) to raise money for charity. It's a brilliant idea – and a pleasant way to spend a Sunday afternoon. See the website: **www.ngs.org.uk**. Details of garden openings are given in an annual publication, The Yellow Book, available from bookshops or the NGS head office.

## Go to the pictures or theatre

Some cinemas put on special programmes for the over 60s or offer them reduced prices on a particular day of the week. Investigate what is available locally. And look out to see what is on at your local theatre. Whether your taste is Gilbert and Sullivan, Agatha Christie, or contemporary drama, your local amateur dramatic group may have just the thing. Ticket prices are usually modest, and there are sometimes special rates for senior citizens.

# Interests & enthusiasms
## Chapter summary

- Make sure you have something you're passionately interested in.

- If you have a partner with common interests, make sure you also have interests of your own.

- Don't be afraid to learn a new skill or take up a new hobby.

- Consider adult learning courses.

- Visit your library to find out what's going on locally.

- Join in local activities that reflect your interests.

- Consider voluntary work.

- Visit museums, art galleries and historic buildings.

- Get out into the countryside.

- Try a music, book or arts festival.

"Another good thing about being poor is that when you are seventy your children will not have declared you legally insane in order to gain control of your estate.

*Woody Allen*

# The roof over your head

# chapter 6
# The roof over your head

"Any old place I can hang my hat is home to me" wrote William Jerome (the American songwriter). Where and how we live is a very personal thing. But for most of us, home means having a place of our own where we are comfortable.

It's not unusual for someone who retires to move to a new part of the country, or to go abroad. There might be good reasons for this. Perhaps you want to move closer to your family? Perhaps your health will benefit from a drier climate? Or perhaps you just want to up sticks and move to a place where you have always wanted to live?

Remember that where you live is not just a question of bricks and mortar. If you're tempted to move, think about it carefully before you take the plunge. Don't be seduced by the estate agents' sales patter. Moving home can be a stressful and expensive business. Make sure it's what you really want to do.

Whether you're planning to move to another part of the country or to buy property abroad, it's a big decision. Consider all the options, and think about the pros and cons.

The grass may be greener on the other side of the fence; before you put your feet down on it, make sure that it's got firm roots.

## Think before you move house

If you're thinking of moving house, think long and hard before you do it – especially if you're planning to move to another part of the country. List all the things you like about your present house and – even more important – your present locality. How many of these things will you have in the place you're planning to move to? If there are some important things you'll have to do without, make sure that these are outweighed by the advantages of the new place.

## Where you live is not just a question of bricks and mortar

If you move away, will you miss your friends and relations? If you have close friends you've been used to seeing once or twice a week, how will you fill that gap? Of course, there'll probably be some people you'll be very pleased to leave behind! But making new friends in a different part of the country might not be easy. You'll need to make a real effort to integrate into the local community. Joining local organisations that reflect your interests is a good way of doing this.

Retirement Wit

*I feel like I'm diagonally parked in a parallel universe.*

**CONSIDER ALL THE OPTIONS**

If, for one reason or another, your present living accommodation no longer meets your needs, take time to think through all the options. And, before you do this, be clear in your own mind about exactly why you need to move.

## Do you ...

... just need somewhere smaller — perhaps in order to reduce your maintenance costs and heating bills and the amount of gardening you have to do?

... need to move to an area where accommodation is cheaper, so that you can release some capital? ... Need to be closer to your children?

... think that moving to accommodation with all the rooms on the same level will make things easier? (Consider installing a stairlift instead of a move to a flat or bungalow.)

... want to live in a quieter environment, perhaps alongside other retired people?

... want to be closer to the shops, or to local train or bus services?

... need sheltered accommodation of some kind, with the presence of a warden? Or nursing care?

Be clear about why you have to move, what your needs are, and how these can best be met. Consider all the options.

## A permanent home on dry land is probably best

If you're going to move home, you probably want to move to a solidly built house or flat that's on dry land! But you might just want to consider more adventurous alternatives. One retired couple I'm acquainted with decided to make a clean break with their previous existence. They sold their house and used the proceeds to buy a comfortable canal boat. They now spend their summer months cruising the waterways of Britain, and their winters moored in a canal basin which is within easy reach of shops and other local facilities.

## Moving house can be very stressful – and expensive

Next to divorce and bereavement, moving home has been shown to be one of the most stressful of all human activities. It also involves substantial expenditure – solicitors' and estate agents' fees, stamp duty (if you're above the exemption limit), removal costs and, probably, some new fittings and furnishings for your new home. Make sure, before you commit yourself, that all the hassle of moving – and the stress and expenditure – will be worthwhile.

## Retirement Wit

*Junk is something you've kept for years and throw away three weeks before you need it.*

## Retirement developments have some advantages

If you've reached that stage of life where you want to avoid property maintenance and gardening, you might want to consider a retirement development. There are many different types, providing different facilities, and at different prices. Such accommodation can give added security and support, perhaps including a resident warden. And you might enjoy the company of others who have similar needs.

## But they are not for everyone

If, on the other hand, you like to mix with a wide range of people of different ages and with different interests, you might be better off staying where you are, or simply moving to accommodation that is not specifically designed for retired people but which frees you from house maintenance and gardening chores.

## Try out your new locality before you make the move

It's a good idea to have a trial run before you commit yourself to buying a house, especially if you're considering moving to a part of the country you don't already know well. You can do this by renting somewhere to live for a short period. If you're captivated by a chocolate-box country cottage you saw in the springtime, or a quaint seaside town you visited in the summer, make a point of going back there in the depths of winter. You'll be in a better position to decide whether you can cope with living there all the year round.

## Some parts of the country are healthier than others

In theory, moving from one part of the country to another could increase your life expectancy. A move from central Glasgow to Surrey, for example, could add around 10 years to your life. In practice, of course, it's not quite as simple as that, for two reasons. In the first place, those parts of the country where life expectancy is high tend to have high property prices. Secondly, your current state of health is the result, among other things, of where you have lived most of your life. So if you've spent sixty-five years of your life in Liverpool or Manchester, you can't expect a retirement move to Dorset or Norfolk to transform your life expectancy overnight.

## Living abroad has its attractions …

There are three main reasons why people decide to move abroad once they've retired: a better climate, the cheaper cost of housing, and a different, more relaxed way of life. It's not surprising that many people who have spent their lives in a country like Britain, with its damp and changeable weather, should head for Southern Europe. The climate is warmer and more reliable (in Italy people have more years of healthy life than anywhere else in Europe). You can probably buy a house a good deal cheaper than you would pay for its equivalent in Britain – though costs vary enormously depending on location. And the chances are that the pace of life will be slower and more relaxed than you've been used to at home.

# And its pitfalls …

If moving to a different part of Britain needs to be undertaken with care, moving abroad needs extra care. The potential benefits need to be weighed against all the things – and all the people – you'll miss. Just how important to you is a warmer climate? How easy will it be for you to settle in a country with different customs and a different language? Try it out for a few weeks or months before you take the plunge.

## Learn the language

There are English-speaking enclaves abroad where you might be able to get by with little or no knowledge of the local language. But to get the most out of living abroad, you'll need to develop at least a conversational knowledge of the language. Then you'll be able to chat to the neighbours and the shopkeepers. You'll find life a lot easier, too, if you have a basic reading ability – so that you can understand public notices, labels on products in the shops, and the headlines in the local newspapers. There's no great mystery about learning a language. After all, French and Spanish toddlers pick their native language up easily enough! They just imitate what they hear. Imitation is the best way to learn any language. Use language tapes, CDs, DVDs. Listen to the radio. Watch television. Language is about communication. It shouldn't be an obstacle course in irregular verbs. Believe it or not, learning a language can be fun!

# Where to live if you want a healthy old age
## Female life expectancy*:

**Best**

| | | |
|---|---|---|
| 1 | Kensington and Chelsea | 86.2 |
| 2 | Epsom and Ewell | 84.5 |
| 3 | East Dorset | 84.1 |
| 4 | South Cambridgeshire | 83.9 |
| 5 | Rutland | 83.8 |
| 6 | Purbeck | 83.7 |
| 7 | Guildford | 83.6 |
| 8 | New Forest | 83.6 |
| 9 | North Dorset | 83.5 |
| 10 | Horsham | 83.4 |

**Worst**

| | | |
|---|---|---|
| 1 | Glasgow City | 76.7 |
| 2 | West Dunbartonshire | 77.5 |
| 3 | North Lanarkshire | 77.6 |
| 4 | Inverclyde | 77.9 |
| 5 | East Ayrshire | 78.0 |
| 6 | Liverpool | 78.1 |
| 7 | Renfrewshire | 78.2 |
| 8 | Halton | 78.3 |
| 9 | Hartlepool | 78.3 |
| 10 | Manchester | 78.3 |

# Male life expectancy*:

**Best**

| | | |
|---|---|---|
| 1 | Kensington and Chelsea | 82.2 |
| 2 | East Dorset | 80.9 |
| 3 | Hart | 80.2 |
| 4 | Uttlesford | 80.0 |
| 5 | Wokingham | 80.0 |
| 6 | South Norfolk | 80.0 |
| 7 | Chiltern | 80.0 |
| 8 | Horsham | 79.9 |
| 9 | Brentwood | 79.8 |
| 10 | Crawley | 79.8 |

**Worst**

| | | |
|---|---|---|
| 1 | Glasgow City | 69.9 |
| 2 | West Dunbartonshire | 71.0 |
| 3 | Inverclyde | 71.1 |
| 4 | Comhairle nan Eilean Siar | 72.1 |
| 5 | Manchester | 72.5 |
| 6 | Renfrewshire | 72.6 |
| 7 | North Lanarkshire | 72.7 |
| 8 | Dundee City | 73.0 |
| 9 | Blackpool | 73.2 |
| 10 | Clackmannanshire | 73.2 |

* Source: Office of National Statistics, 2006, based on local authorities.

Money is a blessing that is of no advantage to us except when we part with it.

*Ambrose Bierce, 1842–1913*

## Don't neglect security

It's a sad fact that the older you get, the more vulnerable you are to crimes by those prepared to take advantage of your forgetfulness or your good nature. Take simple precautions. Make sure your windows and doors can be securely locked. In some parts of the country there are Council schemes that provide for free checking and, if necessary, replacement of locks. Before you go to bed, check your doors and windows. When you're out of the house, make sure that doors and windows are closed and locked. If you're going away, it's a good idea to leave a light on and a radio playing (not too loudly!) and get a friend or neighbour to keep an eye out for any intruders or unusual visitors.

## Be wary of unknown callers

A chain on your front door is a useful precaution. Don't remove it until you are sure of the credentials of the caller. Ask for proof of identity. Don't allow anyone into your home if you have doubts about them. If the caller claims to be from one of the utilities or their sub-contractors and wants to check a meter or examine an installation, keep an eye on them while the work is carried out. Be cautious about any unknown caller who wants to use your bathroom, or asks you to fetch a glass of water; and don't allow an unknown caller into a room on their own.

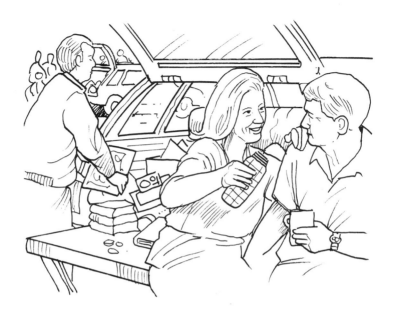

## Don't clog up your house with useless junk

Summoning up the resolve to get rid of useless objects is not always easy — especially, perhaps, when they belonged to your parents or your children, or they're of sentimental value because of particular associations or memories. And most of us need to surround ourselves with at least a few objects which are special to us for one reason or another. But don't go overboard. Remember what William Morris said: "Have nothing in your house that you do not know to be useful, or believe to be beautiful." That's an ideal that most of us might not achieve, but it's not a bad dictum to bear in mind. Car boot sales can be great fun and very rewarding too, so start sorting.

# The roof over your head
## Chapter summary

- Think carefully before you move home.
- Consider all the options.
- Try out a new location before you commit yourself.
- Where you live might affect how long you live.
- A move abroad needs extra care.
- Living abroad has advantages – and pitfalls.
- Take care over security.
- Don't fill your home with useless objects.

At my age I do what Mark Twain did. I get my daily paper, look at the obituaries page and if I'm not there I carry on as usual.

*Patrick Moore*

# The positive approach

# chapter 7
# The positive approach

Let's face it: sooner or later, we'll all be dead. Don't put your head in the sand and pretend it won't happen to you. Accept the inevitable – and turn a negative into a positive by doing your damnedest to make the most of the time you have left.

"Always look on the bright side of life", Monty Python's catchy lyric, is a pretty good rule. It's not always easy, with all the complexities and frustrations of modern life, to put this into practice. But being as positive and optimistic about the future as you can is a good guiding principle. It might even lengthen your life expectancy (a recent study in the Netherlands suggests that elderly men are at less risk from heart disease if they have an up-beat view of the future).

So look forward, not back (now, who said that?). Don't hanker after the past and don't let little irritations about the present get you down. Life in the twenty-first century has a great deal to offer – even if you're an oldie.

## Retirement Wit

*Experience is a wonderful thing. It enables you to recognise a mistake when you make it again.*

## Remember that no-one is immortal

The Victorians allowed no discussion of sex in polite society. Today it's death that is the great taboo. Denial of death – reluctance to think about it or discuss it or plan for it – is an unhealthy modern phenomenon. Accepting the inevitability of your own death is a positive, not a negative, thing: it has two big advantages. First, it acts as a stimulus, encouraging you to make the most of the time you have left – whether that means completing a project that's dear to you, or putting your financial affairs in order, or devoting more time to your family and your friends. Secondly, it helps those close to you to prepare for the inevitable and, when the time comes, makes it easier for them to handle the natural process of grieving and mourning. If you're keen on statistics and you enjoy a tongue-in-cheek look into the future, there is a website (**www.deathclock.com**) that can give you an estimate of the date of your own death!

## Don't spend all day with your feet up

Are you tempted by the image of an old guy in slippers, sitting in an easy chair with his feet up in front of the television? After a lifetime of work it's only natural to want to take things easy. Of course, it's OK to relax. But don't overdo it. The more active you are, both physically and mentally, the more you're likely to enjoy life – and the longer you're likely to live to enjoy it!

# Make good use of your time

When you were working, the shape of your day was dictated by your job. Now you can organise your day in the way you want. It's all too easy to fritter away the time. Try to have a plan. You can divide each day into morning, afternoon and evening – you can even sub-divide these if you really want to! The plan doesn't need to be rigid, and you can always change it if you need to. But if, for example, you reserve one morning a week for routine household chores, one for gardening and another for the weekly shop, you'll be able to earmark the rest of the week for activities you really enjoy.

# Remember the little things

Little things matter. They really do. The objects you have around you in your home. The time you get up and the time you go to bed. The kind of daily routine you have. How you cope with the household chores. How, when, and where you do your shopping. When and where you have your meals. The TV programmes you watch. The newspapers and magazines you read. How you talk to your friends and relations. How you deal with people you don't know. Take care over the little things, and you'll find it easier to deal with the big things: things like illness, financial worries, or an unforeseen family crisis.

## But don't let little irritations spoil your day

Life today can be very irritating. There are so many little things you can get annoyed about, and it's easy to over-react. Of course, there is a time to complain and to react to what's going on around you, but there is also a time to accept the inevitable and to go with the flow. If you know you can't change something, or do anything about whatever it is that's irritating you, there's not much point in letting it spoil your day. Keep a sense of proportion and perspective.

**Quick tip**

**DON'T FEEL SORRY FOR YOURSELF**
There is absolutely no point late in life in feeling guilt about the past or self-pity about the present. They are a waste of time for you — and they are probably very boring for other people. Consign negative feelings to the scrap heap. Count your blessings and focus on the good things in your life.

## Forget the good old days

Don't fall into the trap of constant moaning about the present, and thinking that things were better in the past. Of course, some things were better — some changes have been for the best, and some haven't. But you'll feel more at ease with yourself — and others will find you more interesting to talk to — if you focus on what's good about the present. A positive approach to life is good for you!

In the end it's not the years in your life that count. It's the life in your years.

*Abraham Lincoln, 1809–1865*

## OK, so some things were better in the past

You don't have to believe that everything is better today than it was in the past. Some things were better then than they are now. Your perception of what those are depends on your own background, your beliefs and, dare I say it, your prejudices – we all have them. The trick is to recognise these, but not to dwell on them. It's not difficult to draw up a list of ten things that were better in the past than they are today. Here's my list:

## Tony's top ten – things that were better in the past

- **The railways**
  Before Dr Beeching butchered them and government after government starved them of investment and then privatised them.

- **Post Offices**
  When there were more of them, you could get your TV licence there, and they did not pretend to be banks and insurance companies.

- **Libraries**
  When there were more of them, and they had plenty of books.

- **Television**
  Before it was dumbed down and given over to reality shows and police and hospital dramas.

- **Postal services**
  When there were two deliveries a day and a letter posted one day was always delivered the next.

- Sport in schools
  Before playing fields were sold off.

- Newspapers
  Before they became celebrity-obsessed.

- Local shops
  Before butchers, grocers, and greengrocers were driven out by the supermarkets and the high streets were taken over by chain stores, estate agents, and antique dealers.

- Country bus services
  When they were extensive, reliable and cheap.

- Travelling by car
  When the roads were quieter and drivers were more considerate.

## Compile your own list of things that were better in the past

I'm sure you'll disagree with some of the things on my list. Why don't you have a go? Draw up your own list. Then, after you've looked back and compiled your list of things that were better in the past, why not take a look at the present, and draw up a list of your pet hates? Get it all off your chest. You're allowed some gripes about modern life! Here are mine:

## Tony's pet hates about modern life

- Call centres.
- Telephone sales calls.
- People who share their mobile phone conversations with the rest of the world.
- Junk mail.
- Drivers who tailgate, or ignore speed limits, or don't indicate when they're going to turn left or right or move from one lane to another, or park on double yellow lines, or share their loud music with you, or drive with one hand on the steering wheel and the other clutched to a mobile phone.
- Cyclists and joggers who expect other footpath users, regardless of their age, to give way to them.
- Wall-to-wall music in shops, pubs, restaurants and hotels.
- People eating smelly fast food on public transport.
- Traffic jams.
- Footballers and football managers who argue with the referee.

## But don't dwell on the past

Once you've drawn up your two lists – things that were better in the past, and things that you hate about the present – put them to the back of your mind. Be positive. Admit it: that there are some jolly good things about the present! Draw up a list – and try to make it longer than your two previous lists! Here's mine:

## What Tony likes about today

- Emails, the internet and digital photos.
- Pub opening hours.
- Charity shops.
- Eating out.
- Books and magazines.
- ATMs.
- The Channel Tunnel and Eurostar.
- Farmers' and local produce markets.
- Voluntary work.
- Conservation awareness.

> ## Retirement Wit
> *By the time you can make ends meet, they move the ends.*

## Be tolerant and fair-minded

Tolerance, fairness and sympathy for the underdog are said to be characteristic of the British. Well, some of the people I know are more tolerant and fair-minded than others! And if their favourite Premiership football team is playing non-league opposition, there's unlikely to be much sympathy for the underdog. But it's not a bad idea to be as tolerant of others as you can. Bear in mind that there might just be some rational explanation (or even justification) for behaviour or beliefs which seem indefensible or inexcusable. You don't have to abandon your own principles or beliefs. All you have to do is to avoid making assumptions and judgements about others.

## Listening is hard work

If you want to get the most out of your retirement, you'll need to be able communicate effectively with your friends and relations – and with the world at large. Sounds easy, doesn't it? We constantly speak to one another. But all too often, we don't listen. We switch off. Of course, if the chap you meet in the pub spends an hour telling you his family history and going into enormous detail about his great uncle, who was famous for the prizes he won at the local flower show, you'll want to switch off – or, better still, escape from his company – pretty quickly. That's understandable: we'd all do the same. But if you want to get on with people and build a decent relationship with them, you really do need to listen to what they have to say. And that often requires a conscious effort. It's hard work.

"The past always looks better than it was. It's only pleasant because it isn't here.

*Peter Finlay Dunne, 1867–1936*

## Don't be too judgemental

It's easy to spend time criticising other people. We all do it. Gossip – about our relations or friends or colleagues at work – adds spice to our lives. It's a natural and enjoyable human activity; a part of everyday life. But don't let it get out of hand. If someone does or says something hurtful or malicious, remember that it might be the result of circumstances you know nothing about. Try to avoid being too judgemental about the way other people live or act. Constant carping about the behaviour of others will not make for a contented retirement.

## Retirement Wit

*If you think nobody cares if you're alive, try missing a couple of car payments.*

# Make a little list

Why not make a list of everything you regret not having done with your life? But don't waste time crying over spilt milk or mulling over missed opportunities. Turn a negative into a positive: look to the future. Make a list of all the things you're determined to do before you die. Make sure that some of the items on your list are achievable if you put in the necessary effort – for example, spending so many hours a week learning a new skill or practising a musical instrument. But it's also a good idea to include one or two objectives that are really challenging. For me, these would include writing that best selling novel and (even more improbable) scoring a century for my village cricket team.

# Age has its advantages

"Age is something that doesn't matter, unless you are a cheese", the American actress Billie Burke famously said. Nevertheless, as you get older, life will get more difficult in some ways. You won't be as agile as you once were. Your limbs won't be as strong. Your body will slow down. Your brain will probably work more slowly. You might become forgetful. But there are compensations. Believe it or not old age can bring serenity, detachment, and peace. And as you get older, you can get wiser. It's true – you really can! Old age often gives people perspective and wisdom that those who are younger have not yet had the time or the life-experiences to acquire.

## The early bird catches the worm

As they get older, many people tend to sleep less and to be at their most energetic in the morning. Why not try getting up an hour earlier than usual? You might surprise yourself with how much you can get done during that extra hour. The chances are, you'll be facing the world when you're at your peak.

## Make the most of it

By the time you're retired, you should have learned something about life! You owe it to yourself and to others to make the most of whatever experience, skills, insights and wisdom you have gained. Use what you have learned in the past to make the most of the present. Live life to the full – and enjoy it!

### Retirement Wit

*When Charles de Gaulle decided to retire from public life, the British Ambassador and his wife threw a gala dinner party in his honour. At the dinner table, the Ambassador's wife was talking with Madame de Gaulle: "Your husband has been such a prominent public figure, such a presence on the French and international scene for so many years! How quiet retirement will seem in comparison. What are you most looking forward to in these retirement years?" "A penis", replied Madame de Gaulle. A huge hush fell over the table. Everyone heard her answer … and no one knew what to say next. Le Grand Charles leaned over to his wife and said, "Ma cherie, I believe ze English pronounce zat word, 'appiness!'"*

# The positive approach
# Chapter summary

- Accept the inevitable – you won't live for ever.
- The more active you are, the more you'll enjoy life.
- Plan how you're going to spend the day.
- Don't dwell on the past.
- Count your blessings and focus on what's good about the present.
- Think positively about the future.
- Be tolerant of others and listen to what they have to say.
- Don't be too judgemental.
- Age has its compensations.

# Classic Retirement Syndrome

Ever heard of A. A. A. D. D. – Age Activated Attention Deficit Disorder? No? Oh, I think you have! This is how it manifests itself ...

I decide to water my garden.

As I turn on the hose in the drive, I look over at my car and decide my car needs washing.

As I walk towards the garage, I notice that there is some post in the letterbox.

I decide to go through the post before I wash the car.

I lay my car keys down on the hall table, note that there are some bills to be paid amongst the post and put the junk mail in the rubbish bin under the table. I notice that the bin is full.

So, I decide to put the bills back on the table and take the rubbish out to the end of the drive first as the bin men are coming later.

But then I think, since I'm going to be near the post-box at the end of our drive when I take out the rubbish, I might as well pay the bills first.

I take my chequebook off the table, and see that there is only one cheque left. My extra cheques are in my desk in the study, I go to my desk where I find the can of orange juice that I had been drinking earlier.

I'm going to look for my cheques, but first I need to push the orange juice aside so that I don't accidentally knock it over. I see that the juice is getting warm, and I decide I should put it in the refrigerator to keep it cold.

As I head toward the kitchen with the orange juice, a vase of flowers on the kitchen table catches my eye: they need to be watered.

I place the can of juice down on the work surface, and I discover my reading glasses that I've been searching for all morning.

I decide I'd better put them back on my desk, but first I'm going to water the flowers.

I put the glasses back down on the work top, fill a container with water and suddenly I spot the TV remote control. Someone has left it on the kitchen table.

I realise that tonight when we watch TV, I will be looking for the remote, but I won't remember that it's on the kitchen table, so I decide to put it back in the lounge where it belongs, but first I'll water the flowers.

I pour some water in the flowers, but quite a bit of it spills on the floor. So, I set the remote control back down on the table, get some paper towel and wipe up the spilled water.

Then, I head down the hall trying to remember what I was planning to do.

At the end of the day:
- The car isn't washed
- The bills aren't paid
- There's a warm can of orange juice on the kitchen table
- The flowers don't have enough water
- There is still only one cheque in my chequebook
- I can't find the remote control
- I can't find my glasses
- I don't remember what I did with the car keys.

Then, when I try to figure out why nothing got done today, I'm really baffled because I know I was busy all day long, and I'm really tired. I realise this is a serious problem, and I'll try to get some help for it, but first I'll check my e-mails.

PS. I just remembered, I left the hose turned on ....... !

# Useful web addresses

## Chapter 2 – Health

www.ramblers.org.uk

www.helptheaged.org.uk

www.ageconcern.org.uk

www.heyday.org.uk

## Chapter 3 – Money

www.direct.gov.uk/en/over50s

www.moneymadeclear.fsa.gov.uk

www.readitswapit.co.uk

www.bookcrossing.com

www.mystery-shoppers.co.uk

www.freecycle.org

www.gumtree.

www.free2collect.co.uk

www.letslinkuk.org

www.swapaskill.com

www.TeamUpHere.com

www.U-exchange.com

www.timebanks.co.uk

www.wwoof.org.uk

www.whatsmineisyours.com

www.swapstyle.com

# Chapter 5 – Interests and enthusiasms

www.about.com

www.language-learning-advisor.com

www.readinggroups.peoplesnetwork.gov.uk

www.english-heritage.com

www.cadw.wales.gov.uk

www.chortle.co.uk

www.volunteering.org.uk

www.shapearts.org.uk/shapetickets

www.Geenee.com

www.Homebase-hols.com

www.oybike.com

www.rspb.org.uk

www.wildlifetrusts.org

www.nationaltrust.org.uk

www.ngs.org.uk

# Chapter 7 – A positive approach

www.deathclock.com

**Disclaimer**
*The websites, services and resources listed in this book have not paid for their entries – they are included as a guideline only and the author/publisher does not endorse their products or services.*

# Index

# 'The Greatest Tips in the World' books

*Baby & Toddler Tips*
by Vicky Burford
ISBN 978-1-905151-70-7

*Barbeque Tips*
by Raymond van Rijk
ISBN 978-1-905151-68-4

*Cat Tips* by Joe Inglis
ISBN 978-1-905151-66-0

*Cookery Tips*
by Peter Osborne
ISBN 978-1-905151-64-6

*Cricketing Tips*
by R. Rotherham & G. Clifford
ISBN 978-1-905151-18-9

*DIY Tips*
by Chris Jones & Brian Lee
ISBN 978-1-905151-62-2

*Dog Tips* by Joe Inglis
ISBN 978-1-905151-67-7

*Etiquette & Dining Tips*
by Prof. R. Rotherham
ISBN 978-1-905151-21-9

*Freelance Writing Tips*
by Linda Jones
ISBN 978-1-905151-17-2

*Gardening Tips*
by Steve Brookes
ISBN 978-1-905151-60-8

*Genealogy Tips*
by M. Vincent-Northam
ISBN 978-1-905151-72-1

*Golfing Tips*
by John Cook
ISBN 978-1-905151-63-9

*Horse & Pony Tips*
by Joanne Bednall
ISBN 978-1-905151-19-6

*Household Tips*
by Vicky Burford
ISBN 978-1-905151-61-5

*Personal Success Tips*
by Brian Larcher
ISBN 978-1-905151-71-4

*Podcasting Tips*
by Malcolm Boyden
ISBN 978-1-905151-75-2

*Property Developing Tips*
by F. Morgan & P Morgan
ISBN 978-1-905151-69-1

*Retirement Tips*
by Tony Rossiter
ISBN 978-1-905151-28-8

*Sex Tips*
by Julie Peasgood
ISBN 978-1-905151-74-5

*Travel Tips*
by Simon Worsfold
ISBN 978-1-905151-73-8

*Yoga Tips*
by D. Gellineau & D. Robson
ISBN 978-1-905151-65-3

# Pet Recipe books

*The Greatest Feline Feasts in the World* by Joe Inglis
ISBN 978-1-905151-50-9

*The Greatest Doggie Dinners in the World* by Joe Inglis
ISBN 978-1-905151-51-6

# 'The Greatest in the World' DVDs

*The Greatest in the World – Gardening Tips*
presented by Steve Brookes

*The Greatest in the World – Yoga Tips*
presented by David Gellineau and David Robson

*The Greatest in the World – Cat & Kitten Tips*
presented by Joe Inglis

*The Greatest in the World – Dog & Puppy Tips*
presented by Joe Inglis

For more information about currently available
and forthcoming book and DVD titles please visit:

# www.thegreatestintheworld.com

or write to:

**The Greatest in the World Ltd**
PO Box 3182
Stratford-upon-Avon
Warwickshire CV37 7XW
United Kingdom

Tel / Fax: +44(0)1789 299616
Email: info@thegreatestintheworld.com

# The author

Tony Rossiter is a freelance writer who likes to both inform and to entertain his readers. His published work includes a humorous cricket book and articles in national magazines on subjects as diverse as country walking, public houses, Russian folk art, ferret-racing and collecting litter from National Trust beauty spots. A former diplomat and civil servant, he combines writing with work as a freelance management trainer and international consultant.

Tony provides practical, common-sense information and advice based on his own experience of retirement. He believes that it's very important to have a consuming interest – something you're really passionate about. Tony writes in a simple, direct style which is fun and easy to read.